MEMOIRS RED AND WHITE

To Benjamin Van Voorhees

from

the author, Peter D.

MEMOIRS
RED
AND WHITE

POLAND,
THE WAR, AND AFTER

PETER F. DEMBOWSKI

University of Notre Dame Press
Notre Dame, Indiana

Library of Congress Cataloging-in-Publication Data

Dembowski, Peter F. (Peter Florian), 1925–
Memoirs red and white : Poland, the war, and after / Peter F. Dembowski.
    pages   cm
Includes bibliographical references and index.
ISBN 978-0-268-02620-2 (paper : alkaline paper)
ISBN 0-268-02620-3 (paper : alkaline paper)
1. Dembowski, Peter F. (Peter Florian), 1925–
2. Dembowski, Peter F. (Peter Florian), 1925– —Family.
3. World War, 1939–1945—Personal narratives, Polish.
4. World War, 1939–1945—Underground movements—Poland.
5. Soldiers—Poland—Biography.
6. Poland—History—1918–1945—Biography.
7. Polish people—Canada—Biography.
8. Immigrants—Canada—Biography.
9. University of Toronto—Faculty—Biography.
10. University of Chicago—Faculty—Biography.   I. Title.
CT3150.D46A3   2015
943.8'04092—dc23
[B]
2015017653

To my children, Anna, Eve, and Paul

CONTENTS

PREFACE

After the publication of my book *Christians in the Warsaw Ghetto* (Notre Dame, 2005), I realized that my generation, the generation of the Second World War, was disappearing in an accelerated fashion. This should not have surprised me, but it did, and it led me to add my voice to the others of my generation. The first draft of my memoirs was written for my children and grandchildren. Some readers of that draft suggested that my reminiscences would be interesting to a more general public. In this book I have eliminated certain details of interest only to my family but left the majority of the text intact.

Like the Polish flag, composed of two contrasting colors, red and white, my memoirs are cast in red and white. "Red" treats largely my wartime life in Europe, life full of blood and death. My success in that part of my life was survival. "White" represents my successful migration and peaceful life in America.

Since I believe that I come from an interesting family, I describe its members in some detail. For some facts about my forebears, I consulted the writings of my mother, and for details concerning the death of my mother and my sister, I consulted materials published after 1989. Otherwise, there were no attempts on my part to conduct historical research or to engage the methods of academic writing. I began to write down my memories in the summer of 1998, and after many interruptions, I finished this work in the summer of 2014.

To provide a broader picture of the collective experience of my generation during that calamitous century, I mention my contemporaries as well as the members of my extended family. The experiences of my generation are important to Poland. The postwar Soviet government made considerable attempts to "control" recent history, to make it conform to the official Marxist historical "truth." While these attempts were generally unsuccessful in Poland itself, I think that the Soviet propaganda had some influence outside that country. For instance, the often-repeated opinion that all, or almost all, of anti-Nazi resistance was inspired by the Communists entered more readily into the historical consciousness of the West than in Poland. I hope that my reminiscences will contribute to a more historically authentic picture.

NOTE ON POLISH NAMES AND ORTHOGRAPHY

Customarily, within the family and among friends, Poles use the diminutive forms of first names, given here in parentheses at first appearance. A relatively small number of first names are used, so to distinguish between various persons, many names have several diminutives. Thus Maria can be Marysia, Mania, Mańka; and Anna, Ania, Anka, Anula; and so on. I use these diminutive forms when they seem to be easier to Anglo-Saxon eyes and ears. Thus I write Bronek, Franek, Kasia, Włodek, and so on, rather than Bronisław, Franciszek, Katarzyna, Włodzimierz.

In Polish, c is always ts (even before k); ch is h (horse); w is v; j is y (as in *yet*); y is a short English i (*bit*); cz is ch (*church*); sz is sh; szcz is shch (*ashchurch*); rz is zh (as in the French Jacques). There are three specific Polish vowels: ą is a nasal o, resembling the French *on*; ę is the nasal e, French *fin*; and ó; ó and u are always oo (*tool*). There are five specific consonants: ć (and c followed by i) is a soft (palatal) ts (the Italian *ciao*); ś (and s followed by i) is a palatal s (*sure*); ź (and z followed by i) is a palatal z (*pleasure*); ł is w; ń (and n followed by i) is the Spanish ñ.

PART ONE

"RED"

The Old Country and War

ONE

Family

BEGINNINGS

I was born in Warsaw on December 23, 1925, the son of Henryka (Henia) Dembowska née Sokołowska and Włodzimierz (Włodek) Dembowski. My parents had three children before me: Katarzyna (Kasia), born July 30, 1919, who became Sister Zofia, a Franciscan in the Laski convent near Warsaw, and died there in 2002; Małgorzata (Małgosia), born February 26, 1922, arrested by the Gestapo on May 14, 1941, and executed, together with her mother, in the women's concentration camp at Ravensbrück on September 25, 1942; and Franciszek (Franek), born February 2, 1924, a retired geologist living in Kraków. The youngest member of our family, Bronisław (Bronek), was born on October 2, 1927. He became a priest in the diocese of Warsaw in 1953 and was bishop of Włocławek from 1992 until his retirement in 2003.

Both of my parents came from landowning families of the old *szlachta* class, that is to say, the gentry. The gentry possessed a coat of arms and a long family history, both authentic and mythical. According to Jan Hempel, an ardent genealogist and family member (the husband of the daughter of my great-aunt), the Dembowski family can be traced to the beginning of the fourteenth century.

The *szlachta* class was a specific Polish institution. It should not be confused with the aristocracy, for only the very top of the *szlachta* constituted the true aristocracy. Before the partitions of Poland, at the end of the eighteenth century, the gentry were relatively numerous, constituting 20 percent of the population. They elected the king of Poland (who was automatically a grand prince of Lithuania), and they voted for the members of Parliament (the Sejm). After the last partitions in 1795, they played a leading role in all cultural, social, and national movements. They have been, in fact, a voice of national conscience. In the nineteenth century (above all, after the 1863–64 Insurrection) the *szlachta* class lost much of its economic power.

The descendants of *szlachta* families became the soul of the Polish intelligentsia. The Communists talked about Polish society of the 1940s and 1950s as a post-*szlachta* society, and quite rightly so. To give just one example, Lech Wałęsa, a peasant turned proletarian, talked, looked (his mustache, for example), and acted like a good old member of the *szlachta*; his opponent, General Jaruzelski, the last general secretary of the Polish Communist Party (KPP), was an authentic member of the *szlachta* and acted like one, in spite of his Communist role. The main characteristics of this post-*szlachta* intelligentsia class were a high level of Polish patriotism, absolute devotion to the idea of the independence of Poland, often combined with social and political progressivism, a sense of personal involvement, and a highly developed capacity for improvisation. I was born into this post-*szlachta* intelligentsia milieu.

MY FATHER'S FAMILY

Both of my father's parents were members of the landowning gentry, quite impoverished at the time of their birth. I do not remember my grandfather Aleksander, who died in the early 1930s. He was apparently charming, and, according to my cousin Jadwiga Dembowska, his grandchildren adored him. His brother Bronisław (after whom my brother was named) was a pioneering ethnologist who "discovered" the folklore of the Góral people from the Tatra Mountains region and was the author of a dictionary of the Góral dialect. According to my mother, he belonged to the most creative group of the Polish intelligentsia. In the summer of 2009, a museum originally founded by him in Zakopane was officially opened as a state museum. Bronek, Franek, and Franek's children were guests of honor at this occasion. My grandfather had a third brother, Tadeusz, who was an outstanding surgeon and an active citizen of Vilna (Wilno).

My paternal grandmother, Helena Brodowska, was what we used to call "a brave Polish woman." She came from an important but impoverished family. Her father, Ludomir Brodowski, was dean of the Medical Faculty in Warsaw and an accomplished researcher. Helena was totally devoted to her children, three daughters, Hanna, Aniela, and Stanisława (Stasia); and three sons, Kazimierz (Kazik), my father, Włodzimierz (Włodek), and the youngest, Stefan, who drowned in the Vistula River when he was a boy.

My grandmother was given to social causes, or, as Poles called voluntary involvement in neighborhood associations, *praca społeczna*, literally, "social work." In independent Poland she became a school principal and always remained an ardent Polish Socialist, and therefore anti-Stalinist. I knew her well, because during the 1938–39 school year I lived in her tiny apartment in Warsaw and spent time in Hanna's and Stanisława's households. At the beginning of the war my grandmother was ill with cancer. She went to live with her son Kazik and his wife, Janina. I was living with them, too, and I assisted my grandmother in her last weeks on earth. She loved her children and grandchildren, but she was far too possessive and not easy to get along with in daily life.

My father's sisters remained ardent leftists throughout their lives. Hanna and Aniela were Communist sympathizers, and after 1945, in their old age, they became (unimportant) Party members. The youngest sister, Stanisława (Stasia), was a non-Communist leftist and late in life became an ardent Catholic.

My brother Bronek told me that when he attended Hanna's funeral he carefully covered his Roman collar with a scarf as the few people present were aged Communists. The funeral was of course nonreligious, just a speech or two and the singing of the

Internationale. Sad, old, trembling voices on a gloomy Polish winter day, chanting about the "last struggle" that would save mankind, convinced Bronek to add his priestly baritone to the chorus. A true example of charity.

I remember all three of my paternal aunts as very strong but also quite bizarre. I believe that they were taught by their mother to be emancipated vis-à-vis the male of the species and the rest of the world. Their mother was not only a Socialist, but an early and devout feminist (the late nineteenth-century Polish term is *emancypantka*, "an emancipated woman"). Each of her three daughters, after having produced two offspring, immediately divorced their husbands. Such behavior was most unusual in 1930s Poland. Like their mother, Hanna, Aniela, and Stasia loved their children with the passion and possessiveness of a mama grizzly bear.

Hanna had two sons with her husband, Mieczysław (Mietek) Kwiatkowski. Mietek had a passion for automobiles and for Communism (in that order), but he made his living, not very successfully, by translating American Westerns into Polish. In September 1939 Mietek found himself in Soviet-occupied territory and quickly realized that the NKVD (People's Commissariat of Internal Affairs) was not the same as the pre-1939 Polish police. The latter knew of his membership in the outlawed Communist Party, and they used to arrest him routinely in honor of May Day on April 30 and release him on May 2. The NKVD was far more serious: it was arresting members of the Polish Communist Party and killing them as "deviationists." Mietek went into hiding and died soon after, of some disease probably caused by constant fright.

I knew his sons, Piotr and Andrzej, very well. During the war, they had the rare distinction in my extended family of being the only ones in my generation, to my knowledge, who did not participate in any clandestine organizations. Their mother tried to ensure that they remained far from danger. They were even kept away from the rest of the family, suspecting, quite rightly, that we were involved in all sorts of anti-German clandestine activities, for which I shall use here the Polish term *konspiracja* (meaning "conspiracy" but without a pejorative connotation).

To describe one's clandestine activity, the Poles used to say that one was "in *konspiracja*" or "in *organizacja*." During the occupation, everybody's desire was to have good papers, legal if possible, proving that they were working in an institution approved by the Germans. The people in *konspiracja* often had better papers than others. People without papers were frequently caught in the great street and house roundups (called *łapanki*) organized by the Germans and sent to forced labor in Germany.

In 1943, I think, Hanna found perfect work for her sons: they became members of the Żolibórz (a northern suburb of Warsaw) fire company. As firemen, they had good papers, warm uniforms, and wonderful sheepskin coats. Their work protected them from German conscription into working on behalf of the occupiers. Little did they know that by 1944 most of the members of the Żolibórz fire company were a part of the regular secret army unit of the Armia Krajowa, the AK (Home Army, lit., "Army of the Country," as opposed to the Army Abroad). Early in 1944 there was a breakdown in AK security, and despite the sounding of an alarm (prepared in advance precisely for such an emergency) warning everyone to stay away from the fire station, some members of the group were arrested.

The Kwiatkowskis were among the very few unaware of the situation, and they were promptly arrested by the waiting Gestapo unit when they arrived to begin their shift. By sheer chance, on May 3, 1944, I met Andrzej in the courtyard of the Warsaw prison. He was a yard "trustee," and I was waiting in the yard to be freed from the prison. He told me that the Germans were particularly rough on him because his mother had stenciled the letters "AK" (Andrzej Kwiatkowski) inside his coat, neither she nor he realizing that it stood for Armia Krajowa. Her ignorance of the letters AK shows her complete isolation from the society in which she lived. As suspects, both boys were sent later to a truly horrible camp, Stutthof, near Danzig. They survived, but, as they say in French, *à peine*. Liberated by the Russians, they joined the reigning Communist Party and made nice careers in the People's Republic of Poland.

My aunt Aniela, a trained physicist, was arrested with my mother and spent three years in Ravensbrück. In her memoirs, written from a distinctly Communist point of view, she never mentions my mother by name, only once referring to her "sister-in-law," and she never speaks of my sister Małgosia. There is a typical Polish irony in this story. Aniela wanted to have her memoirs published in Poland, but apparently the officials of Communist Poland did not find it orthodox enough, so her son Stanisław had to have it published in London at an émigré, basically anti-Communist publishing house.

The August 1944 Warsaw Uprising took the life of Aniela's son Kazik. He was my favorite cousin. A little older than I was, he was strikingly handsome and dark like a gypsy; he resembled a Hollywood star. His older brother, Stanisław (Stach), survived the Uprising.

My other aunt, Stasia, married a prominent sculptor, Franciszek Strynkiewicz. She lost her daughter Agnieszka, called Jagoda (Berry) within the family, in the Uprising. Like her father, Jagoda was a talented artist. The younger daughter, Barbara, survived the war.

Neither my father nor his older brother Kazimierz (Kazik) shared the unusual behavior of their sisters, which was a mixture of eccentricity and egocentricity. (This, of course, was my view as a young, and therefore censorious, fellow.) Kazik received some scientific training in Paris before 1914. All his adult life, Kazik taught physics in secondary school. Until the war he taught in the secondary school run by his wife, Janina Landy. My *stryj* (many Poles distinguish between the paternal uncle, *stryj*, whose wife is *stryjenka*, and any other uncle, called *wuj*) Kazik was one of the most selfless persons I have ever known. He was also a model husband. Very witty but shy and kind, he was loved by his students. During the war, when the Germans closed all schools in Poland, he participated in clandestine teaching (*komplety*, lit., "assemblies"), small groups of students (about six in number) who met in private apartments for regularly scheduled classes. Janina's high school continued such activities until the Uprising, and Kazik became a member of a sapper group.

Let me give an example of Kazik's fertile mind. In about 1942 I was ill with a nasty flu and sleeping on the couch in the same room in which Kazik was giving a physics lessons to five young ladies (living conditions were abominable). He explained in great detail the principle of an artificial satellite circling the earth. All we need, he said, is a great cannon (he had served in the artillery in 1920) to shoot the satellite far enough from earth's gravity. I remembered his lesson when the Russians launched their first Sputnik in 1957.

Kazik married Janina Landy in 1917. She and her two sisters were important figures in my life. The members of the Landy family, established both in Poland and in France, were nonreligious Jews involved in commerce. Janina loved to tell me a legend that illustrates the character of her family. In 1862–63, during one of the many anticzarist manifestations, the Cossacks fired at the crowd, killing the man at the front, who was bearing a cross. Janina's ancestor Michał Landy, marching behind the fallen man, picked up the cross and continued the march. He too was fatally shot. Talking about it in 1968, Janina considered this an omen of her conversion.

Janina and her sisters, Zofia and Henryka (called Dzidka, "the Baby"), became Christians. Their brother, Adam, whom I never met, became an ardent Marxist. Like many members of the KPP, Adam went to the USSR and was executed, in about 1936, in the purges of Polish Communists for their "deviationism." He was, as Janina proudly told me, rehabilitated by the Polish Communists in the 1970s.

Their mother, whom I remember very well as a sweet little lady, was called *babcia*, "granny," by everyone. She was full of life and good humor. She did not become a Christian but got along extremely well with both her Christian and her Communist children. She was caught and killed by the Germans in one of their many roundups in Warsaw in, I believe, 1943.

Her youngest daughter, Dzidka, was far more French than her two older sisters. She spent her entire youth in France and in Poland became a superb teacher of French. She was perhaps too strict as a teacher. I still remember the fear of making a mistake in French in her presence. She and Janina were very influential in my choice of studies and profession. In 1962 Dzidka approved of my French. *Quelle victoire!*

During the war Dzidka was an important member of the Underground. She and her future husband, Martyniak (a one-armed Polish officer who was parachuted in from England), started a clandestine manufacturing operation producing hand grenades, called *filipinki* (from Martyniak's pseudonym "Filip," Philip). Officially, it was a factory making carbide lamps, which required heavy metal containers. My brother Franek worked in the factory, both as a sworn member of the *konspiracja* and as a paid employee.

Dzidka survived the German occupation but was arrested by the Polish Communists, accused of communicating with the Polish government in exile in London. She and her husband were sentenced to long terms in prison. They were released, before November 1956, during the first "thaw." Dzidka returned to teaching French.

It was Janina who played an especially important role in my life. After the death of my father, she became my second mother, and after the arrest of my mother and the news of her death, she was my only mother. The Landy sisters had distinctly Semitic features, easily recognizable as such by the local population. Unlike her sisters, Janina was beautiful. In a photograph taken in her youth she looks like the Old Testament Sarah painted by a Pre-Raphaelite. She remained beautiful even in old age. Like her sisters, she was an ardent person—an ardent Christian, an ardent patriot, and an ardent educator.

Many people knew about Janina's Jewish background, including one of her former students whose family became *Volksdeutsch*, that is, a self-declared ethnic German, or a supposedly ethnic German, who acquired provisional German citizenship. Declaring oneself *Volksdeutch* was practically the only way of being accepted by the Germans, who considered other Poles racially inferior. Janina told me after the war (one did not discuss such matters during the occupation) that she was never threatened with denunciation. She was a tower of strength, endurance, and love. It is likely that, after the death of my mother, I owed my mental health to Janina's love. I also owe to her my interest in the Polish Jews.

The eldest of the three Landy sisters, Zofia, became a serious theological scholar. I remember her teaching a lesson on the virtuous Susanna to Grade 6 boys in the school for the blind in Laski. When she started talking, the boys, most of them blind, forgot their sniffles and giggles suggested by the subject, but I had the feeling that the Old Testament was speaking to me directly. Zofia was doubtless the leading force in the Christianization of the Landy sisters. A big, round woman, she was an intellectual and a personal friend of Jacques Maritain and his wife, Raïssa (like the Landys, a Jew by birth). In the early 1920s she became Sister Teresa in the Laski convent.

My mother's sister Zofia Sokołowska, a young sculptress of some renown, and several other outstanding young women, many of them of Jewish background, were the founders of both the Laski convent and the Institute for the Blind. The leader of the Laski movement, Mother Czacka, was born with an incurable progressive eye disease and became totally blind in her early twenties. She decided to establish a Franciscan convent for the blind and in service to the blind. At the same time, the organization in Poland also became a movement of Catholic renewal working with the educated classes.

In the course of the nineteenth century, many members of the Polish intelligentsia became either indifferent or inimical to Christianity. They had just discovered science, progress, and rationalism, and they considered religion part of obscurantist folklore, good enough for the common people but certainly insufficient for those who had become enlightened. The Laski movement squarely faced the challenge, as my mother used to say, of the "rationalistic error." The movement has had a profound influence on the development of Polish Catholicity. It suffices to say that Karol Wojtyła, the future Pope John Paul II, was a follower and friend of the great Laski figure Cardinal Wyszyński, who himself was influenced by the adviser and cofounder of the Laski movement, Fr. Władysław Korniłowicz.

Janina and Kazik had two daughters, Jadwiga (Jadwisia) and Anna (Anula). Jadwiga was a geologist, and another very strong person. When I lived with Kazimierz and Janina in 1940–42, I was a little afraid of her. I viewed Jadwiga and Anna as beloved sisters (in Polish, one can to refer to a first cousin as "sister" or "brother").

Jadwiga entered the *konspiracja* early in the war. She was enlisted by her boss and her fiancé at the Institute of Geology. Early in 1942 she was arrested by the Gestapo. She had entered a "burned" apartment, that is, an apartment discovered by the Gestapo. The Germans were lying in wait to arrest all who entered. Jadwiga must have had a reasonably good (nonconspiratorial) excuse for going to the apartment, for she was not killed but sent to Auschwitz (or more precisely, to the women's part of Auschwitz, Birkenau). Her tattooed camp number was 25979. She survived by a miracle, really by the miracle of the devotion of her fellow prisoners.

During the evacuation of Auschwitz in 1945, somebody saw Jadwiga lying on a little cart often used to transport dead bodies. Jadwiga's "death" was reported to her fiancé, who promptly married her best friend. Jadwiga returned from Germany shortly after their marriage. The wife was a difficult, high-strung, unhappy person. Jadwiga was an "aunt" to their children and took care of them after the early death of their mother. She died in February 2004, after several months in a semicoma, leaving behind a life of fidelity, devotion, piety, and toughness.

Anna had always had a medical vocation. She started regular medical training during the occupation. Of course, it was illegal, for the Germans closed not only all the secondary schools but also the universities. However, they did allow practical nurses' training. Anna's class, directed by a distinguished professor of medicine, was, in fact, given regular medical training. She obtained a doctor's diploma right after the war, when such training was certified by the surviving members of the teaching team. (My 1944 secondary school diploma is of that kind.)

Immediately after the war, Anna met, while hitchhiking, Władek (Władysław) Rodowicz, a former Majdanek and Auschwitz prisoner and before that an important member of the *konspiracja*. As she says, "This was love at first sight. How can you possibly resist this shaven head and this smile showing lots of missing teeth lost during the Gestapo interrogations?" Władek was a genuine hero of the 1939 war and of the *konspiracja*. He spent more than two years in the Majdanek and Auschwitz concentration camps. He and Anna married in the summer of 1945, and Bronek was a witness at their wedding. They had many children, Jan, Tomasz (Tomek), Piotr, Maria (Marysia), Anna, and Antoni (Antek), and many grandchildren. Anna died in March 2007 of complications from a stroke, and Władek died in the fall of 2013.

MY FATHER

My father, Włodzimierz (Włodek), was born on June 29, 1892, on a small property in the Russian part of Poland. Soon after his birth, his parents sold the land and moved to Warsaw, where my grandfather ran his small teamster business. During the Revolution of 1905, when he was thirteen years old, my father participated in the youth revolutionary activities of the Polish Socialist Party (PPS). He was encouraged in this by his mother and sisters.

In 1912 Włodek entered the secret Polish military organization called the Riflemen (*Strzelcy*).The organization was legal in Austrian Poland but illegal in the Russian empire. The name "Riflemen" itself goes back at least as far as the 1863–64 Insurrection. In the fall of 1913 Włodek spent some time in the czarist Pawiak prison in Warsaw (built in 1835). I would get to know the same prison building in April and May 1944.

Later, I believe, my father went to Paris to study. At the beginning of World War I, Warsaw and most of Russian Poland was occupied by the German-Austrian forces. Józef Piłsudski, a former Socialist activist and czarist prisoner, created the Polish Military Organization (Polska Organizacja Wojskowa, POW) to fight on the Austrian side. (By the end of the war, there were Polish troops in the German, Austrian, French, and Russian armies.) In the former Russian zone, the POW began semilegal (and many illegal) activities. My father came back to Poland and in 1915 joined the

Warsaw Battalion. He was sent to the Russian front. On October 2 of the same year he became a Russian prisoner of war. Fortunately for him, the Russians did not realize that before the war he had been a subject of the czar; he would have been shot as a traitor.

My father twice attempted to escape. Finally, after the Russian Revolution, and after months of hunger and wandering, like many Polish soldiers of the Russian army and like many prisoners of war, he joined the Fourth Regiment of the Polish Riflemen, organized in Mohylev in Belarussia. The war on the eastern front was ended by the German-Bolshevik treaty of Brest-Litovsk in 1917, but the German army occupied all of Poland and the western territory of Belarussia and the Ukraine. My father, weak and sick, came to Poland in the summer of 1918.

In 1917 and 1918 the young Zofia Landy was a live-in tutor for my mother and her four younger sisters at my maternal grandfather's estate, Biejkowska Wola. My father's brother Kazik was already married to Janina Landy. My father, quite naturally, went there to recuperate from his Russian adventures, and thus he met his future wife.

On October 26, 1918, he married the eldest daughter of the house, Henryka. I am convinced that theirs was a love match. They loved each other, and they certainly loved their children, in spite of their differences: my mother was profoundly Catholic (reconverted to the faith by Zofia Landy), while my father could not accept a personal religious commitment. He had always been scrupulously ethical; like many of his generation, he was living the ethical heritage of Christianity without realizing it. But there was absolutely nothing antireligious in his attitudes. Before the marriage, he promised my mother that he would participate in the Christian upbringing of the family. He always observed this promise, in fact and in spirit.

After the marriage, my father worked in the offices of the newly constituted Polish Parliament, but when the Polish-Soviet war became perilous, with the Bolsheviks at the gates of Warsaw, my father volunteered, on August 3, 1920. He had already reached the rank of corporal (my rank in August 1944) in his previous military service. On August 15 the Polish armies carried out a decisive victory over the Red Army, led by Trotsky and his political commissar, Stalin. Four days later, my father received a saber wound in the head from a Red Cossack. As a medievalist, teaching in an era of mechanized war, I often think about my father's wound, so much like the wounds of the heroes of medieval romances and chansons de geste.

After his recuperation, my father decided to stay in the army as a professional soldier. To serve in the reconstructed "real" Polish Armed Forces was for him a patriotic duty and a personal honor. He went to the Officer Training School and spent the years 1920–36 as a sublieutenant and lieutenant in the educational services of the Polish army. From 1929 to 1936 he was a regional officer in western (formerly Prussian) Poland, in the Międzychód district of Poznań, as co-coordinator of the voluntary military preparedness units and of physical fitness training.

At the beginning of 1936 my father asked for a transfer to the Border Guards, which was trying to control petty smuggling from Germany. It was a paramilitary organization run not by the army but by the Ministry of Interior. He became a senior commissioner of the Border Guards in Grajewo, Białystok district, on the border of Poland and East Prussia. At the same time, however, he discovered that he had a heart condition. He died suddenly on the morning of February 19, 1937, after suffering a heart attack the previous night. He had not missed one day of his beloved service.

My father, Włodek, was a friendly person, appreciated for his humor and funny stories. Quite small of stature, his charges often called him "our little lieutenant." He was scrupulously honest and took his duties seriously. He also loved animals, a trait all his children inherited. Our family once owned a Siamese cat (a rare thing in those days in Poland) who adored my father and climbed on him and descended ceremoniously, head down, as if he were a tree. One cold night, my father brought home a half-frozen porcupine. It spent the winter with us. I remember that at home my father was occasionally short-tempered, a condition doubtless caused by his heart disease. But I also remember his kindness.

MY MOTHER'S FAMILY

Henryka (Henia) Sokołowska was born on April 22, 1893, on an estate belonging to her mother's family, Brzeźce, in the district of Radom. She was the eldest daughter of Wojciech (Adelbert) Sokołowski and Stefania née Bagniewska.

I regret not having known my maternal grandfather, Wojciech Sokołowski, who died in October 1939. Shortly after his wedding he acquired a small estate, Biejkowska Wola, that he developed into a modern semi-industrial farm. He retired from farming in about 1922, separated from his second wife (Stefania, his first wife, had died), and took care of his youngest daughter, Maria (Myszka). The estate was given to the second youngest daughter, Anna, since my mother and her sister Barbara were committed Socialists, not suited to take over its operation, and Zofia was already in the Laski convent.

My maternal grandmother, Stefania, died many years before I was born. According to my mother, she was a fine woman, with real and deep sentiments but without sentimentality. Throughout her life she struggled against sadness. I believe that she was affected by incipient tuberculosis. My mother would talk in some detail about her mother's religion, an important factor in view of her own reconversion in about 1917. Stefania Sokołowska was profoundly religious and at the same time alienated from the church. This situation was not uncommon in Poland in the second half of the nineteenth century.

My grandmother had artistic abilities and an artistic temperament, which her daughters inherited. She died soon after the difficult birth of her youngest daughter, Maria. All her children were still young at the time. My mother was convinced that had my grandmother lived longer she would have freed herself from the "superstition of rationalism."

My grandmother had three brothers, Leon, Michał, and Bogusław. Leon inherited the family estate of Brzeźce, and Michał settled on a neighboring place, called Szczyty. Bogusław was an engineer in Warsaw. His son Michał (Michael) moved to the United States.

At the beginning of the war, when my mother found herself penniless and menaced by a local *Volksdeutch* woman, she took us to Brzeźce. Like everybody else at that time, she thought that the war would last only a few months.

I spent the first year of the war in Szczyty. Leon's and Michał's houses were filled with refugees, some from the territories incorporated into the Reich, some from the East, which was occupied by the Soviet Union on September 17, 1939. The Bagniewskis' generosity was remarkable. Fortunately, the war brought unexpected prosperity to farmers: the prices of food, notoriously low before the war, quickly shot up.

Still, the arrival of their niece Henia and her five children, aged twelve to twenty, must have been a difficult burden to bear. Leon's wife, Maria, made sure, and not subtly, that we would not feel at home in Brzeźce. My younger brother, Bronek, was the only one who spent the entire war there. He was treated shabbily. He lived and ate with the servants, who were very kind to him, especially the gardener. This probably saved my brother from arrest in 1944, when Leon was sent to a German concentration camp. Bronek told me that Maria spoke to him after he became a priest, when she was old and sick. She was fully cognizant of her bad treatment of him and tearfully asked his forgiveness.

In Szczyty, I was welcomed by Michał's wife, Lucyna, an odd person and an ardent animal lover and vegetarian. My position as a shepherd in Szczyty gave me the feeling that I was not an intruder, not a poor relation. Toward Brzeźce, I maintained the lofty attitude of an offended prince and never visited them. Of course, my princely pride went unnoticed. But I shall always remember the Bagniewskis from Szczyty with gratitude.

Michał and Lucyna had two sons, Tadeusz (Tadzinek) and Jerzy (George). The former was a trained agronomist, a staunch vegetarian, and a lover of women. He was married to Grażyna, who was the closest thing in our extended family to a member of the oldest profession. Tadeusz was a big, fat, lusty guy whom I called uncle, although he was my cousin twice removed.

Tadzinek's story is typical of many lives in the land of my birth. I suspect that he was involved in the *konspiracja*, which was more difficult in the country than in the city. In any case, he was arrested by the Germans in 1942 or 1943 and sent to Auschwitz. Grażyna immediately settled into a blissful union with an ugly *Volksdeutsch*, the newly appointed administrator of the estate. I saw her for last time in the summer of 1944, when the "boys from the forest" (partisans) came and shaved her head.

After the war Tadzinek went to work on the nationalized farms (Państwowe Gospodarstwo Rolne, PGRs). But the PGRs were from the start a total failure. Like many things in the post-1945 era, they were social experiments conducted with a total disregard not only for common economics but also for common sense. Later, Poles called Stalin's and the post-Stalin economic system a "moon economy." State farms were expensive pools of the unemployed, and almost all ran a deficit during the Communist period.

Tadeusz was fired from a few jobs and finally arrested. He was sent to a Communist concentration camp and spent several years there. He came back a broken man. He settled down with a solid second wife and forgot his "colorful" behavior. When I saw him in the mid-1980s I did not recognize him: he was thin, small, bent over, and withdrawn. Seeing me, he asked Bronek, "Who is this handsome gentleman?"

His younger brother, Jerzy, was my good friend. He trained to be a merchant marine officer but, curiously, became a reserve officer candidate in the air force. In 1939 his unit was assigned to build temporary airfields. He was captured by the Soviet army and sent to an officers' internment camp at Starobielsk. Fortunately for him, the Germans asked their Soviet friends and collaborators to hand over some of the Polish prisoners. Jerzy, apparently like other members of the air force, was in that number. They traveled in boxcars, and when they reached German-held territory they realized that they were not being guarded very carefully. The prisoners, except for Jerzy, jumped from the train as soon as it slowed down. Realizing that the train would pass close to Szczyty, Jerzy waited until it got closer to the familiar station, then jumped, and a half hour later was at home.

Jerzy was very lucky, for thousands of Polish officers from the Starobielsk camp were found later in the graves at Katyń. The massacre took place in May 1940, though it was not until 1990 that it was acknowledged by the Russian government.

Jerzy, a quiet and phlegmatic fellow with a distinct technical bent, got into the local *konspiracja* in the communication branch. This was especially dangerous work since radios had been confiscated by the Germans, and possession of a receiver or transmitter was punishable by death.

Sometime in 1942 I was with Jerzy in Warsaw, waiting for the bus to take us to his home, which was some thirty miles away. A group of security police (*Schutzpolizei*) stopped us to examine our papers and look through our belongings, a common occurrence during the occupation. Jerzy had a briefcase full of small radio parts, which, he quietly explained to the Germans, were toys. Not being fluent in German, he used the Polish word, *zabawki*. The Germans looked perplexed, so I, always a snob about knowing languages, blurted out, "*Spielzeugen.*" The Germans left, whereupon Jerzy, wiping the perspiration from his face, for the first and last time in our relationship broke the rule of the *konspiracja*. "Those are radio parts, you know," he said. Had I known that beforehand, I would have stifled my urge to show off my knowledge.

This brave man was apparently very shaken by the post-1945 regime. He sailed in the merchant marine for several years but was afraid to get in touch with his relatives. According to Paweł Matuszewski, a cousin who met him only briefly in London, Jerzy was completely terrorized. This loyal citizen of the Polish Democratic Republic lived in constant fear of being treated like his brother. He died in the 1970s, still afraid.

There were five Sokołowski sisters: my mother, Henryka (Henia), Barbara, Zofia, Anna, and the much younger Maria (always called Myszka, "Little Mouse"). Myszka suffered an injury during birth and remained sickly throughout her life.

Anna, pretty and full of life, was the heiress to the estate, but she was obliged to pay her sisters a considerable sum of money calculated in dollars, for the early 1920s were a time of runaway inflation in Poland. Anna married (eloped with, I believe) a charming but otherwise frivolous chap named Michał Matuszewski, who through speculation lost the estate of Biejkowska Wola during one of the first busts of the 1920s. I did not know about Anna's debt to my mother, but it came to play an important role in my life.

Anna Matuszewski had two children, Paweł (Paul) and Maria-Józefa (Marjózia). Marjózia was charming and delicate but with an inner strength. At home she was called Felek (the diminutive of Felix), a nickname she took as her *konspiracja* pseudonym. She performed distinguished service in the famous Battalion Zośka (a diminutive of Zofia), composed chiefly of former Boy Scouts, which in 1944 fought in the Old City. After the war Marjózia became an art historian, but like many former members of the AK, her career was thwarted by the Party. Puciata, her husband, although certainly of *szlachta* origin, became a Party member and left his Catholic and AK wife to further his career. Like her mother, Anna, Marjózia died of cancer, in November 1978.

Paul was, like me, in the AK in the Baszta Regiment. His pseudonym, not terribly original, was Paweł. His company took part in the Uprising close to where my squad was positioned. Later, we were in the same barrack in the Stalag. Paul was a small fellow who tolerated hunger better than most of us. He was therefore more cheerful. He also was fond of practical jokes, and on one occasion he poured water into the pocket of a fellow who was asleep. After the war he settled in London, where he became either a pharmacist or the owner of a pharmacy. I visited him in London in 1953, and he came to Paris to be a witness at my wedding. He died of cancer in London sometime in the 1970s.

My aunt Barbara married an architect, Stanisław Brukalski, and she herself became an architect. Her husband spent the war in a prisoner of war camp for officers. I remember him as a giant of a man, handsome, and holding original views on architecture. Barbara and Stanisław had four sons, all too young to be in *konspiracja*. Józef died in France in 2007. His brothers, Jan and Baltazar, both became architects. Baltazar worked abroad during the Communist regime. His salary, paid in dollars, was shared with the Polish government. Jan remained a faithful friend of my brother Franek. He died in October 2011.

Myszka, the youngest of the Sokołowski sisters, was placed in an institution for not quite "autonomous" adults, and my grandfather, like many of the other parents, had a little cottage next to the institution so that he could be with her. In September 1939 Hitler ordered the elimination of "useless persons." It was a quintessential Nazi idea: "modern," "rational," and "scientifically" eugenic. It was the "final solution" applied to people who were sickly or disabled.

In the first days of the German occupation, at the beginning of October 1939, the patients in the institution (and their relatives who lived nearby) were executed. In occupied Poland this law was carried out with brutal logic. All the patients in the state hospitals were killed. Wojciech and Myszka Sokołowski were shot by the German police sometime in the second half of October 1939. After the war a list of those who were executed was found.

Now follows a truly strange and very Polish situation in my life. I learned about the killing of Wojciech and Myszka Sokołowski only in Chicago in the late 1980s, when Anna Matuszewska's grandson Greg was living with us. Greg invited his former nanny, whom he had always called "aunt," to Chicago. In her youth Stefania (Stefcia) was a housemaid at Biejkowska Wola, and she had remained close to Anna and her family. (A good Marxist would have to exercise quite a bit of ingenuity to understand such attachments, not at all uncommon in the Poland of my memory.) After Anna's death, Stefcia took care of her daughter Marjózia. After the untimely death of Marjózia, Stefcia took care of her only son, Grzegorz (Greg), and it was she who really brought him up. Stefcia knew the history of the Sokołowskis and spoke to me about the deaths of Wojciech and Myszka as if I already knew. At first we were not told about the deaths of our grandfather and aunt because of the basic rule of the *konspiracja*: do not tell anyone anything unless it is essential. In this case the rule made sense, as the Germans treated the next of kin of their victims very harshly.

But there were other, less rational reasons for the silence after the war. My mother was dead and so could not have explained to me the fate of her father. Barbara and Anna probably kept silent because of the place where Wojciech and Myszka met their deaths, Tworki, the biggest state hospital in Poland. In addition to people like Myszka, Tworki housed many genuinely mentally ill people. Poles, I believe, have always had a deeply rooted prejudice or, better, sense of shame concerning the mentally ill or mentally handicapped. The very name Tworki would suggest that Myszka was "crazy." That she was not seems now to be beside the point. I, of course, was hurt by this silence, and I resented those who kept silent, but all of them (including Kasia) are dead.

MY MOTHER

My mother, Henryka (Henia) Sokołowska, was certainly the most important influence on me. Her life and death must be described in some detail here.

My memories of her are those of a child, and I remember her above all as a caring, loving person. She was able to create a warm and welcoming home for us. In 1930, when my memories begin, she was a vegetarian, a stance she abandoned during the war, when you ate whatever you could find.

I know many of my mother's attitudes and feelings, not only directly, but also from her writing. She was a talented writer. Bronek published her fragmentary journal (Włocławek, 1997), miraculously saved from destruction, along with original poems, her translations of Paul Claudel's poetry, and reminiscences by her children and her former fellow prisoners in Ravensbrück. Bronek titled it *W radości i cierpieniu* (In Joy and Suffering).

My mother was a strong person, motivated by her religious convictions. Her religion was deepened by the influence of Zofia Landy. She lived by the principle that being is more important than having. One of her unusual characteristics was that she discussed everything (except her father) with us as if we were adults. Let me quote here from my reminiscences published by Bronek in his book.

I do not remember my mother very well. I cannot recall any important, single scene in which she was a main character, but I remember a mass of simple, everyday happenings, like fragments of a half-forgotten old film. In my mind, I still see her face, and especially her eyes, dark, wise with understanding and full of love. I remember that she always spoke to me as if I were an adult, but I can hardly recall any specific subject of our conversations.

What I have inherited from my mother is the memory of love. I have always had an absolute conviction that I loved her and that I was loved by her. I have never held any belief in my life with more certainty than that love. When I look back on the last seventy years of my life without her, I realize that it was her love that charged me with the energy of love. Her love made me capable of loving my own family.

My mother gave me not only love, but faith in love, this faith, which like faith in God is a grace, that is to say, a freely given gift. She was, above all, an intermediary of the grace of love and faith, and it was through her that this grace flowed down on me and, I believe, on her other children.

Since I wrote those words I have remembered at least one conversation that I had with my mother sometime at the beginning of the war. She told me that it was most important for a man like me (I was about fifteen years old) to find a good wife. One indication that a woman will be a good wife is the fact that she is liked and respected by other women. My mother made me promise that she would be duly consulted in the choice of my life companion. I tried to consult her in my prayers, and it worked out very well, because my wife, Yolande Jessop, was everything that my mother would have liked to see in her daughter-in-law.

Until February 1937 my mother was busy taking care of her family and being active in voluntary social and charitable work. This *praca społeczna* was for her a serious involvement, and badly needed, since our small town of Międzychód in western Poland, like the rest of the country, was in the grips of the Depression. My mother's work outside the home was made possible by the fact that the daily housework was done by our old servant and retainer, Wiktoria Paszewka ("Wikcia" to all of us, because it is diminutive and friendly, but "Wikta" to Franek, who fought her systematically, because it is augmentative and unfriendly).

A word about Wikcia. She was a landless peasant from the poor district south of Kraków. And she was another strong woman in my early life. Though she had little education, she was able to read. But she never abandoned her village views and prejudices. The golden era of her life was pre–World War I, and she spoke with reverence about the good old days of Emperor Franz Josef of Austria. She had no use for the present. She taught us traditional village songs, many of them full of double meanings.

Wikcia always had a marked preference for Bronek (Bronuś to her) and told me incessantly that I had "an evil brown eye" (*bure oko*). She stayed with us up to the beginning of the war, when my mother simply could no longer pay her. Having a live-in maid did not mean that we had a high standard of living. Before the death of my father, we were far from rich, but we had a steady income. It was normal for people like us to share room and board and a modest salary with a servant. Wikcia's beloved Bronek kept in touch with her in later years and attended her funeral. He told me that she had saved all the money from her meager salary, and in 1939 she had enough money in her Post Office savings account to buy a little piece of land, which she had dreamed about all her life. Unfortunately, her savings, like all prewar Polish money, became worthless.

The Depression got worse in Poland. In first grade in 1932, our teacher often asked us during the roll call to recite our family name, our Christian name, and our father's profession. Most of my classmates responded, "*bezrobotny*," unemployed. The teacher, my first true love, patiently instructed them to say, "a worker, temporarily out of work."

My mother was a member of the Women's Association for Civic Work (ZPOK), which took up many good causes. When hundreds of kids began to come to school hungry, she became very active in the St. Vincent de Paul Society and organized regular food services in the school. At eleven o'clock each morning, poor children received a big bowl of soup (milk boiled with wheat flour and sugar) and a chunk of rye bread. For many of them, this was probably the only good meal of the day. I was jealous of their soup, just as I was ashamed that my father was not *bezrobotny* but an officer.

I also remember that at the beginning of my schooling many kids spoke only French. They were children of Polish miners expelled from France, and perhaps Belgium, because they were unemployed. Since my mother had taught me quite a bit of French, I began (in a very humble way) my interpreting activities, which I have been destined to carry out most of my life.

Indeed, my mother represented the spirit of Saint Vincent, especially his precepts of feeding the hungry and clothing the naked and praying that the poor would forgive the charity rendered unto them. Saint Vincent was very practically minded, and so was my mother.

In her *konspiracja* work in 1916–18 and 1939–41 she took the pseudonym "Marta" (Martha), the practical sister of the more "spiritually minded" Mary (see Luke 10:38–42). I have no idea what my mother was doing in the *konspiracja*, but I presume that she was a courier, carrying messages between centers.

She lived in Brzeźce but made frequent visits to Warsaw, where her main clandestine activities took place. On her return trips from Warsaw she carried illegal publications, weekly papers set in small print in a small format. There were many such publications of different shades of political opinion, but the most important for us was the *Biuletyn Informacyjny* (Information Bulletin), expressing the view of the Polish government-in-exile and its clandestine representatives in Poland

The last time I saw my mother was in the second year of the war, on May 14, 1941, in the evening. I was living then with Kazik and Janina Dembowski, and my mother asked me to walk a couple of blocks with her to Aniela Sierakowska's apartment because she had missed the bus and had to spend the night in Warsaw. We were in a hurry, because the German-imposed "police hour," or curfew, was approaching. She did not tell me, of course, that she had a packet of the *Biuletyn* in her small suitcase. I kissed her good-bye and went back to Janina's place.

My sister Kasia told me, many years later, what happened that night. I think that she learned those facts from Aniela. A Jewish woman used to be registered as a tenant in Aniela's apartment, before the establishment of the ghetto in 1940. During the night of May 14–15, 1941, German police came to inquire routinely about this tenant, or more probably to check if she was still there. They found my mother and suspected that she was the person they were looking for. While establishing her identity (*Grundsätze*), my mother, to prove her identity, mentioned her daughter Małgosia and her address. Everything seemed to be going more or less normally, until one of the policemen decided to look through my mother's suitcase and found several *Biuletyns*. My mother and my aunt Aniela were immediately arrested. Małgosia was arrested in the apartment of a second cousin and great friend of my mother's, Wanda Gawecka, in Żolibórz, on Karpinski Street. (I would be arrested in the same apartment 2 years, 11 months, and 23 days later.) My mother must have suffered greatly, blaming herself for the arrest of her daughter.

The facts concerning the concentration camp and the death of my mother and sister were recorded by their fellow prisoners at Ravensbrück and published cautiously under the Communist regime. I say "cautiously" because the Communist rulers of Poland maintained, almost up to the late 1970s, the fiction that only the Communist underground was worthy of having a place in history. The non-Communist underground activities—in fact, the vast majority—were treated at first as anti-Communist, or at least potentially so. After the war the Communists arrested many former anti-Nazi underground fighters, like Dzidka and her husband, mentioned above.

After 1956 the former non-Communist anti-Nazi underground fighters were treated with more indulgence but still as if their wartime activities had never happened. Thus only after the fall of Communism in 1989 could the former prisoners speak and write freely about their wartime experiences.

For the first two weeks after their arrest, my mother and Małgosia were kept in miserable, overcrowded conditions in a quarantine block of the women's part of the main Warsaw prison, called Pawiak because it was situated on Pawia Street. The prisoners were then transferred to "normal" cells, but the adults were separated from the "juveniles" (those under the age of twenty-one). During the first few weeks, both my mother and Małgosia were interrogated several times at Gestapo headquarters, in the former Polish Ministry of Education on Szuh Avenue. They came back to Pawiak badly beaten. Their fellow prisoners tried to help them by applying cold compresses to their swollen faces.

My sister spent the summer of 1941 in "Serbia," the unusual name of the juvenile section of Pawiak. On September 22, many juveniles and a large group of adults were transported to the women's concentration camp Frauen Konzentrations Lager (FKL), Ravensbrück, some seventy kilometers north of Berlin. My mother, my sister, and Aniela Sierakowska were in this transport. At FKL juveniles and adults were not separated, so the three women spent the last twelve months of their lives together in Block 13. My mother's concentration camp number was 7855; my sister's, 7856.

After a couple of weeks of quarantine, my mother worked inside the camp, and Małgosia worked outside the camp, either in the fields or in the forest. The work *na aussen* (a Polish-German hybrid for "on the outside") was hard, but occasionally the prisoners were able to steal and smuggle in some food. In concentration camps there was always a lack of food, but in 1941 and 1942 there were periods of extreme hunger. It is very difficult to describe to people living in normal circumstances what real hunger is. (I went through it myself from the beginning of October 1944 to late April 1945.)

My mother is remembered by one of the witnesses as the discoverer of a method for fighting hunger: she recited food recipes from memory. She did indeed have a good memory and a passion for teaching. She is also remembered as one of the prisoners who taught Polish literature in the camp, recalling in considerable detail the content of the classics. Polish women—constituting the largest national group in the camp—did a great deal of teaching, which was, of course, a clandestine activity. Małgosia taught German to her fellow prisoners, and several older prisoners, professional teachers, offered all sorts of primary and secondary school subjects.

Aniela taught physics, and my mother taught Polish history in addition to literature.

The huge twentieth-century system of concentration camps, both German and Soviet, was based on a perverted legal underpinning. All the prisoners in Ravensbrück were sentenced by some secret SS tribunal in Berlin. There were, as a rule, only two sentences for "political" prisoners, and practically all the Polish women in Ravensbrück were ipso facto "political": life imprisonment or death. Sentences were kept secret. Those sentenced to death only learned of it right before their execution. The others learned they had received a life sentence only after their liberation.

A few words about the camp itself. The bulk of the camp was constructed of wooden barracks with a barbed-wire enclosure and a high wall that prevented the prisoners from seeing the outside world. It was constructed next to a small lake quite close to a charming town. At the entrance to the camp there was the Bunker (a regular prison building made of concrete), a concrete execution tunnel, and a crematorium, the ashes from which were dumped into the lake. The tunnel was about four feet wide, six feet high, and twelve feet long. It was open on one end and barred by a heavy, solid wood door on the other. The persons to be executed were put into the tunnel, and each was shot by a single bullet in the back of the head. The door was opened, and the bodies were removed to the nearby crematorium.

Ravensbrück was occupied by the Soviet army in early 1945. By then, most of the women had been evacuated to Sweden by the personal intervention of a Swedish diplomat, Folke Bernadotte. Until 1989 the camp could not be visited, because the Soviet army was stationed in its buildings. After the Soviet retreat the barracks were destroyed, but the Bunker, the execution tunnel, and the crematorium remained and were turned into a memorial museum. Each of the cells is now a memorial room to a different nationality. The Polish cell has a German record book containing the names and the numbers of Polish prisoners, as well as many photographs of executed women, including those of my mother and Małgosia.

During the especially long evening *Appell* (roll call) of September 24, 1942, the woman vice-commandant of the camp, the *Appell-führerin*, and a female SS officer (probably from Berlin), accompanied by a cadre of SS women, stopped in front of Block 13 and called out six numbers and names, including those of my mother and Małgosia. Immediately after the *Appell*, five of the women were taken to the Bunker. Małgosia's *aussen* group, however, was as usual late for the evening *Appell*. As soon as she was back in her block she gave some smuggled apples to her friends, who told her that her mother and four other women had been taken to the Bunker.

The friends, many of them from the old juvenile section of the Pawiak prison, knew, of course, that this meant execution during the morning *Appell*. Małgosia was allowed to spend the last night of her life with them. They were impressed by her calm and fearless attitude and remembered it well. They spent a sleepless night, and Małgosia spoke freely to them about her life before the war, about her studies and her work in the *konspiracja*, for now it was safe to talk about her personal involvement in it. She told her friends that she was not afraid to die for Poland. You must try to understand that patriotism in the camps was very intense. It was a genuine and deeply felt common bond, but it was also necessary for personal reasons. It protected the prisoners from the dehumanization and feeling of worthlessness that were deliberately and systematically induced by their captors.

Małgosia was taken to the Bunker before the morning *Appell*. The condemned were apparently stripped of their clothes and given paper sacks to wear. While they were waiting for execution, one of them wrote a little note and placed it in her clothing, knowing that it would be sent to the clothing stores operated by the prisoners. The note was found a few days later and passed to the women in Block 13. It said (as cited from memory, many years later), "We are awaiting death calmly. If you survive, you will work for the country in your own and our stead. Long live Poland!" It was signed by all six women being held in the Bunker. During the morning *Appell*, six shots were heard. Two of them ended the lives of my mother and my sister.

In the summer of 1998, my wife, Yolande, Bronek and his chauffeur, and I visited Ravensbrück. The sights, particularly of the execution tunnel, were truly moving. So were the stark inscriptions in all the European languages. There is a simple plaque in Polish, the translation of which states, "40,000 Polish women and girls were imprisoned here; 200 were executed by shooting, 74 were subject to experimental medical operations, several thousand died of exhaustion and disease or were finished off by injection, 8,000 survived until the liberation."

The four of us were speechless with pain and horror. As soon as we left this place, Bronek and his chauffeur started to pray, and Yolande and I joined them. We drove toward Berlin, passing two towns bearing the names of two infamous concentration camps for men: Sachsenhausen and Oranienburg. Bronek told me that, through the efforts of people like him, the Ravensbrück museum became, in April 1997, a center of Polish-German reconciliation.

I believe that in October 1942 a German uniformed policeman came and told the people who were occupying Aniela's apartment that Henryka and Małgorzata Dembowski had been executed. If I remember correctly, my family was not ready to believe this information. But I had noticed that no postcards from Ravensbrück came after September. The prisoners could write in German one postcard a month. Before that time we had received several cards from my mother and from Małgosia. Invariably, the card from one was in the handwriting of the other, to show us that they were together. The cards were heavily censored. I still have one of the envelopes from Ravensbrück. It was from Henryka in Małgosia's handwriting.

I remember one such card that my mother sent to Kasia. It said that she had left her watch with such-and-such watchmaker to be repaired. I went to see him and showed him the card. He found the repaired watch, but when I asked him how much I owed him, he said something like, "In a situation like this, nothing." You cannot imagine how moving this gesture of a stranger was in 1942, and still is. During difficult times, simple gestures of solidarity from a stranger become crucial. They confirm the necessary belief that humans are indeed human.

By 1943 I began to believe that the execution had indeed taken place, and during my own stay in Pawiak prison I became convinced that my mother and my sister were dead.

MY SIBLINGS

My oldest sister, Kasia, was born in 1919. Her godparents were two Jewish Christians, that is, Jewish converts: Zofia Landy and the artist Franciszek Tencer. In the 1930s Kasia was mostly absent from the family. She had a bone disease in one leg and spent long periods in a hospital in Poznań. She returned when she was in high school. Since she was six years older, I did not have much contact with her. I remember that she received her high school diploma (*matura*) in 1938. In about 1938–39 she stayed with my mother in the town of Warka, south of Warsaw, where my mother had just received a concession for a wholesale tobacco store. Tobacco was a government monopoly, and my mother received this concession as a partial reward for my father's meritorious service. It took her many months to gather all the affidavits necessary to obtain a pension for my father that would reflect his service before Polish independence. This was a typical Polish bureaucratic situation. You had to prove the service to the state when the state did not exist. (My generation went through the same process.)

Kasia helped our mother by working as a saleswoman in the tobacco store. She was planning to go to the university to study pharmacology, but the war interrupted her plans. During the war Kasia lived for a while with our mother in Brzeźce, but soon she became a village teacher. She received gifts of food in lieu of a salary. She was liberated by the Russians at the beginning of 1945 in Brzeźce. Very early in July 1946, I believe, she began to think seriously about entering the religious life at the Laski convent. She became a novice in August 1947 and took the religious name Zofia, in memory of her aunt Zofia Sokołowska, whose name in religious life was Katarzyna. Sister Zofia took perpetual vows on August 15, 1954.

Kasia was an excellent nun. She completed her university education, receiving an MA in philosophy from the Catholic University of Lublin in 1959, and worked chiefly as a teacher. For several years she worked with a bright girl who was born deaf and blind. Kasia taught her to communicate with hand signals, and later the girl learned to read Braille.

My wife and I visited Kasia a few times in Laski, and she impressed us as being a happy and serene person. She communicated with Yolande chiefly by smiles and signs, because Kasia's only foreign language was German, but I believe that she understood quite a lot of French.

What impressed me during the Communist regime in Poland was that Kasia, although living apart from the society, was better informed about the social, political, and economic situation than most of the Poles I met during those times. She was a naturally intelligent and good person. She died on December 28, 2002, bragging that her brother from the United States was coming to see her. I arrived in Warsaw a few hours too late. After her funeral two young sisters told me that they had decided on a religious life because of their teacher, Kasia.

The young Małgosia was in fact our boss. Serious and studious and energetic, she certainly ran my life. She strenuously disapproved of the fact that I did not read all the time and found it scandalous that I read my first book only in the second grade. My mother decided that I should be prepared for first communion together with Franek. He was nine and I was seven at the time. The first confession sometimes took place before the first communion. I distinctly remember that Małgosia (then eleven) not only helped me to examine my conscience and made me list my sins to her first, but after one of my confessions she checked, item by item, whether I had told the priest everything. Once I must have missed something, for she sent me back to the church to tell the priest the forgotten sin. I did, because we simply had to obey her, even if her "help" was strictly against religious regulations.

In one of the reminiscences of Małgosia's prison and concentration camp colleagues, the author says that she remembers Małgosia chiefly as a serious person. I realize now that this was indeed my sister's basic characteristic. Because Kasia was unwell and often absent, Małgosia was essentially the eldest child in the family. I shall always remember her reading in a half-reclined position on the couch and drinking herbal tea with an inevitable cat sleeping on her knees. She controlled the cats with the same ease that she controlled Bronek and me. Franek was close to her in age, so he maintained a more independent, or rather a more rebellious, attitude toward her. Małgosia was the most rapacious reader that I have ever known. She read always and everything. She was an excellent high school student. She finished high school in the spring of 1939, and during the first year of German occupation she began to take philosophy courses at the clandestine university. In my last conversation with her, right before her arrest, she was reciting formulas of logic with obvious enchantment.

My brother Franek is older than I am by some twenty-two months. In the fall of 1937 he passed the entrance exam for the Military School (Korpus Kadetów), a distinction offered chiefly to officers' sons. He spent two years in the Korpus in the small town of Rawicz, close to the German frontier. I was very proud of his handsome uniform and quite envious of him. In the summer of 1938, I also tried to be accepted into the Korpus but was unsuccessful. Later, Franek was out of school for a time, and as a result he found himself in the same class at the "half-legal" school, which I will describe later. I think that we spent a year together there. In 1941, I believe, he obtained a place in the Orphanage (Bursa in Polish) in Warsaw run by the only Polish social agency allowed by the German authorities, the RGO (Rada Główna Opiekuńcza, or Main Welfare Council).

Franek joined the *konspiracja* before I did. His pseudonym was "Dzwonek" (Little Bell). Like me, he was recruited in the Orphanage. I spent only one academic year there. At the end of the 1942–43 school year the director of the institution decided for security reasons to get rid of all the boys aged seventeen and older; as he rightly suspected, all of them were by then members of the *konspiracja*. Franek found a place to live in the poor Warsaw district of Wola and worked full-time in Dzidka Landy's clandestine hand grenade factory. He remained there almost until the August 1944 Uprising. Dzidka always spoke of him with the utmost respect. He was, according to her, brave, reliable, and absolutely trustworthy. Dzidka was not famous for being generous with praise. Her opinion mattered.

Franek and I were in the same company during the Uprising. We met at the end of September, in the sewers trying to get to the city center. We were captured together and sent to the same POW camp. I remember one detail of our common experience. When we were out of the sewers, surrounded by gendarmes who had just shot a few of us, Franek proposed that we should shout something patriotic before being shot. I agreed with him, but I was too tired to talk or even think about it.

After a while Franek went to another camp, in Austria. In the last moments of the war he was saved by the German commander. Himmler had given the order to execute the prisoners rather than surrender them to the Allies. Fortunately for Franek, in April and May 1945 some of the German soldiers hesitated to carry out the most outrageous orders. In the end, the German commander marched his prisoners into neutral Switzerland.

After the war, Franek stayed in France, in a Polish military establishment, and obtained his high school diploma. He returned to Poland sometime in 1947 and with Janina's help began to study geology at the University of Warsaw. He did not get a research position in the Warsaw Geological Institute because he refused to conceal his wartime service in the AK. He spent all his years as an industrial geologist working for the Kraków office of the ceramic industry. He married a colleague, Zofia Borejko. They have two children, Bogna and Slawomir (Sławek). Sławek Dembowski married Jolanta, Polish for Yolanda. I consider this an extraordinary coincidence, for Yolande and Jolanta are not common names in Canada and Poland. Sławek and Jolanta have three children, Katarzyna (Kasia), Michał, and Krzysztof (Krzyś). Franek's wife, Zofia, died on November 11, 2009. At the time of this writing (2014), Franek is living in the good care of his daughter, Bogna, a lawyer and notary.

Bronek (Bronisław) is a little less than two years younger than I am, but until the late 1960s I considered him a child. I was quite surprised that in 1964 he was a priest and a trained philosopher and everybody considered him a serious adult. The reason, of course, is that I remembered him chiefly as a younger sibling. After our father's death we spent the 1937–38 school year in Laski, in a small guest house in the forest. We lived more or less alone and attended the school for the blind that year. He was ten at the time, and I was twelve, and the memories of that time established in my mind the fact that Bronek was just a child.

Bronek and I parted company in the fall of 1938. He remained with our mother in Warka, and I went to Stefan Żeromski High School in Warsaw. After the outbreak of the war, Bronek remained in Brzeźce, and I worked at the neighboring Szczyty for a year. Bronek's situation was not an easy one. As I mentioned, he was treated more or less like a servant and lived in the servants' quarters. His particular friend among the servants, the chief gardener, became a *badylarz*, a market gardener, after the war. This business was tolerated by the Communist regime. He supplied vegetables directly to Warsaw and was therefore relatively rich. Now more than ninety, he has remained Bronek's friend.

Bronek was taking classes in the underground high school in the local district town of Białobrzegi and at the beginning of 1944, as a sixteen-year-old, joined the local AK unit, the 72nd Regiment of the Radom Region. His pseudonym was "Szary" (Gray). During the Uprising, his unit attempted to come to aid Warsaw, and Bronek spent a few weeks running in the forest. However, as he told me, nothing much could be done. After the Uprising the Radom group quietly disbanded, and after the war Bronek joined his godmother, Janina, in the south of Poland. He got his high school diploma in Mościce near Tarnów, where Janina had found a teaching post. Bronek wanted to become a priest, but Janina convinced him that in order to be sure of his vocation, he should first obtain a university education. In 1946–50 he studied philosophy at the University of Warsaw, where one of his fellow students was Leszek Kołakowski, then an ardent Marxist. Their divergent views did not prevent them from becoming friends.

Immediately after obtaining his university degree, Bronek went to the seminary, and on August 23, 1953, he became a diocesan priest. His first two posts were close to Laski. When the Warsaw Old Town Church of St. Martin was partially restored in 1956, the archbishop of Warsaw, Stefan Wyszyński, assigned it to the Laski Franciscan sisters and named Bronek its rector. Bronek remained in that post until 1992, when he became bishop of the diocese of Włocławek.

I went to the Episcopal Consecration ceremony and learned there that Bronek is not the first Dembowski to be the bishop ordinary of Włocławek. Antoni Sebastian Dembowski, an important statesman in Poland, was the bishop there from 1737 until his death in 1763. He was married and had several sons, one of whom is our ancestor. In 1729, after the death of his wife, he became a priest and soon was consecrated a bishop. Very few Catholics can boast of being direct (and legitimate) descendants of a bishop.

From the beginning of his priesthood, Bronek participated in many different activities. He was pastor of the blind at St. Martin's Church and convent in Warsaw, chaplain for the Franciscan sisters in Warsaw, and church assistant (chaplain) of the Club of Catholic Intelligentsia, which would become an anti-Communist group.

As a priest, he became one of the early animators of the ecumenical movement in Poland. During the times he spent with us in Chicago, 1969–70, 1975–76, and several weeks in 1985, he became acquainted with the Charismatic Renewal movement in our St. Thomas the Apostle parish in Chicago. In October 1976 he established a prayer group of the movement at St. Martin's Church. He organized other Charismatic Renewal groups and in 1984 became the movement's official pastor in Poland. In 1991 he became a member of the International Catholic Council of the Charismatic Renewal. During the suppression of Solidarity, Bronek was vice-chairman of the Primate's Committee for the Aid of the Arrested and Interned, an important post housed chiefly at St. Martin's. His capable assistant was Władek Rodowicz. In October 2006 both men were honored with the highest civilian decoration, the Golden Commandership of the Order of Poland's Restitution, by the president of the Republic of Poland.

In addition to his multifaceted religious duties, Bronek has had a solid academic career. He obtained a PhD in 1961 and his habilitation (which involves writing another dissertation to enter university teaching) in 1969. He was a professor in the Catholic Theological Academy, where he taught philosophy.

During the Party cleansing of "heretical" Marxist professors, including Kołakowski, Bronek was for a time the only professor in Warsaw who taught nineteenth-century philosophy, including Marxism. Since under Communism every student had to pass a general examination in Marxist thought, many nontheological students came to study with him in the Theological Academy. This was one of those insane People's Republic situations: a priest preparing students from various fields of study for a required examination in Marxism.

Willy-nilly, Bronek was involved in political action against the Communists. From May 24 to May 31, 1977, in the week preceding Pentecost, a group of eight people, later increased to fourteen, began a hunger strike at St. Martin's Church. They were objecting to the imprisonment of workers for their attempts to protest the rise in food prices. The hunger strike garnered enormous public interest. Hundreds of people visited the church to take part in religious ceremonies. Bronek's stubborn, patient, but always prudent actions contributed to the victory of the strikers: the imprisoned workers were freed. This is one of the earliest examples (in Poland in any case) where citizens' pressure changed the position of the Communist authorities. We did not know it then, but the 1977 hunger strike at St. Martin's was the harbinger of the Solidarity movement and of the collapse of Communism in Poland.

I know Bronek was ready to be arrested, because I received in Chicago a memorandum that Bronek sent through an unknown friend traveling to the United States in which he described the day-by-day happenings of the strike and included all his public statements and sermons. He wrote a note explaining that the true account of the strike should be known, because if he was arrested all sorts of falsehoods about his role would be spread by the Communist authorities. Fortunately, he was not arrested.

Bronek was a member of the "Round Table" talks in 1988 at which the Communist authorities debated the opposition over the future of Poland. The Round Table agreements led to a new election and in 1989 realized the peaceful demise of the Communist regime in Poland.

Sometime in the 1970s Bronek received from John Paul II, his former teacher, the title of monsignor, that is, papal prelate. The pope waited for the fall of Communism to promote Bronek to the rank of bishop of Włoclawek. He did so in 1992, and Bronek remained in that post until he reached the retirement age of seventy-five in 2002. In his retirement he has been quite active in various pastoral and religious assignments. It would take a large book to describe Bronek's role in Communist and post-Communist Poland. Such a book, I am sure, will appear one day. With all his achievements and honors, Bronek has remained a simple and humble person, endowed with the saving grace of a sense of humor. The sixtieth anniversary of his priesthood was celebrated with great pomp in Warsaw Cathedral in the summer of 2013.

T W O

Life before September 1939

Let me move back in time. As I said, I was born in Warsaw at home, just before Christmas 1925. I am one of the very rare natives of Warsaw who can boast of and point out the house of their birth. Mine was on Solec Street, and it is still standing. It was apparently overlooked by the German army engineers who blew up every large building in the city after the Uprising of 1944.

As a foreshadowing of my nomadic life, right after my birth we moved to Ostrów Komorowo, where my father was an instructor in gas warfare at the Officer Training School and where Bronek was born. In 1928, I believe, we moved to a little village, Bukowina, in the Tatra Mountains. My father was posted to Poznań, but because of the international fair in the city at that time, there were no apartments to be had there.

I do not recall many things that happened before the war, but what I remember is very clear in my mind. The photos from the Tatra Mountains period show me in the company of a beautiful white, shaggy sheepdog, Wiernuś (diminutive of *wierny*, "faithful"). Everybody told me that he saved my life the time I tried to crawl into the road when the rare car was passing by. Wirnuś apparently stopped me by hanging onto my shirt. Poor Wiernuś later had to be destroyed because he began to kill sheep—a fatal habit for a dog in sheep country.

I must have retained some unconscious memories of my early childhood, because when we came to our summer place at Les Eboulements, in the Charlevoix region of Quebec, I was profoundly attracted to the hilly landscape between Les Eboulements and Saint-Hilarion. I believe that this extraordinary attraction is the result of a vague memory of Bukowina. Bronek told me that the landscape of Charlevoix does indeed resemble the Tatra Piedmont (Podhale).

My real memories begin in the small town of Międzychód in western Poland. We moved there in 1929. One of my first images is that of a group of strange-looking men on railroad tracks going nowhere: three kilometers west there was a German frontier, and that particular line ended in the town. I was told that these men were unemployed (*bezrobotni*), and that word sent a feeling of dread to my heart. The other thing that frightened me was the presence of Germans. You did not see them in church, because in our part of the world Germans were Protestant. Only much later I met somebody who was called *Deutsch-Katholik*. What an extraordinary thing, I thought.

As the westernmost town in prewar Poland, Międzychód had a considerable German minority, but the relations between "us" and "them" were more or less correct. I know that after 1939 they worsened, thanks to the official Nazi *Herrenvolk* propaganda and practice. I remember a little Baptist chapel. One Sunday while returning from Mass, I heard strange voices singing very strange hymns. I was frightened by them, but my mother, always an ardent ecumenist, assured me that they were Protestants, that is to say, Christians praying to God.

In order to get to the market square we had to go down a narrow street that both Germans and Poles called Strantz Gasse (Strantz Lane), because at the end of it lived old Mr. Strantz, who was quite insane. He often shouted at passersby, and the other kids and I were afraid of him. My mother was not, and she explained to me that the poor old man was like that because of his horrible war experiences as a German soldier on the western front.

The linguistic situation in the town of Międzychód was complex. We knew quite a bit of the German language, not directly from our German neighbors, but rather from the autochthonous Polish population, who, while sticking to their Catholicity and their Polishness, had lived with Germans for many generations and knew their language.

We were newcomers from what had been Russian Poland before World War I, and we were, generally speaking, disliked by the autochthons. They called us *hadziaj* (from the Russian *hoziain*, "master"). This dislike did not concern us kids. As during our Tatra times, I quickly learned to talk like the local kids and was therefore accepted by my companions. My father fought against our occasional Germanisms: "Do not play in *Maybergi* but in May Hills," and so on. In fact we used many German (or partly German) words without suspecting their provenance. The real Germans did not attempt to speak Polish unless absolutely necessary, and we spoke to them in German.

I remember going to the market with my mother. At the weekly market, women from the country sold their produce: butter, eggs, vegetables. My mother invariably addressed the ones wearing hats in German (Polish women wore kerchiefs). Transactions conducted in German with the hat wearers were short—"Wieviel kostet?" (How much?)—but much more protracted in Polish with the babushka wearers.

I was occasionally ashamed of my mother's *hadziaj* Polish but never of her German. The Poles in Międzychód certainly maintained their Polish but considered knowledge of German an accomplishment to be proud of. My sister Małgosia, in the last months of her life, was teaching her fellow prisoners German, because knowing the language of your enemies makes survival more likely.

During my childhood, my ears were full of endless discussions about the economic crisis. We got our first radio sometime before the war. Hearing bad news was an everyday experience. The big thing was fear of the Soviet Union. I distinctly remember one of my mother's acquaintances saying to her, "What will happen to us if the Bolsheviks come?" But the Germans were closer. Since we lived three kilometers from the border, we occasionally heard gunfire. This was just before Hitler's time. My father told me that the gunshots came from revolutionary fighting between the Communists and their opponents. He also told us that the Germans were quite orderly people. They worked all week and made revolution only on Sundays.

In the second month of the war, October 1939, in Brzeźce, one of the local German boys from Międzychód, now in a Wehrmacht uniform, recognized my mother. As a former neighbor he was quite friendly, and he knew Polish. If I remember correctly, he had gone to Germany to seek work and was promptly drafted into the army. But there was little of the Nazi in him. He asked my mother whether "Herr Dembowski" had survived the Polish campaign and seemed sorry to hear that my father had died in 1937.

In 1932 I went to Grade 1 of the local public school. Our school was an enormous, to me at least, red brick Prussian building. On one of the walls there was a mosaic of the town crest: a pear tree floating above the river Warta. I understood later the meaning of the crest. Instead of Międzychód (Passage Between [two lakes]), the Germans called our town Birnbaum, "Pear Tree."

In Międzychód I remember falling in love with my classroom teacher, who was very young and very beautiful. She was courted by a big, fat music teacher whose name I still remember: Pan Przewoźny (*pan* = "mister"). I hope that Mr. and Mrs. Przewoźny were not murdered by the Germans in 1939. In areas like Międzychód that were incorporated directly into the Reich, many Polish teachers were killed outright.

I got to know many poor people and impoverished families, most of whom remembered better days before the crisis. My mother organized a soup kitchen for poor kids, in particular, children of Polish immigrants from France.

I remember that once when I was visiting with my friends, the Bombas, I heard horrible stories of want, particularly from their uncle. His words were so bitter and violent that I was afraid of him. I thought that he was losing his mind. I do not know what happened to my friends the Bombas. As native Poles in the territory incorporated into the German Reich, they were probably drafted into the German army, not as Germans, but as "members of the German nation" (*Angehörigen der deutschen Nation*, or *Angedeutsch*). I hope they survived the war.

My happiest memories from the early 1930s are associated with Sieraków. As district commander of military preparedness and physical fitness, my father organized a summer camp in the beautiful lake district at Sieraków, some fifteen kilometers from our home. There were many young people, both boys and girls, living in tents in a pleasant pine forest. Our family had a place a little bit outside the main camp. We had several tents: one for our parents, one for the kitchen and Wikcia, and several small tents for us. I shared a tent with Bronek. Kasia was not there because she was not well enough. I do not remember Małgosia well from our summers in Sieraków because she stayed mostly with the female campers, but I do recall that she swam very well.

In 1936 my father went to be trained as a captain in the Border Guards. I remember that he was quite upbeat about it; it was a real promotion for him. That summer we moved to Grajewo in north-eastern Poland. We lived in an apartment for local civil servants in a small block built by the czarist authorities. That year in Grajewo was a happy time. I was in Grade 5, and Bronek was in Grade 3. I had many friends in school.

It was in Grajewo that I first encountered Jews on a daily basis. I did not see them in school. The Jewish kids went to an old school built by the Russians; the non-Jews, to a new school built by the Polish authorities. But we all played football together. I was a fanatic soccer player in those days.

I believe now that the separation of the Jewish kids in their own school was not a forced ghettoization but rather insisted on by the Jews themselves, who wished to preserve the cultural and religious identity of their offspring. Generally speaking, Jewish-Polish relations in Grajewo were fairly good. The younger Jews spoke Polish (and Yiddish) and participated in many civic activities, for instance, voluntary military preparedness. The older Jews, especially the older women, spoke very little Polish. The Jewish population in that part of Poland was destroyed by the Nazis in the late summer of 1942. Most of the Jews were murdered at Treblinka.

I was a star student in my class because I could read aloud much better than the other students. On February 19, 1937, the school director came to my class and called me to his office. Bronek was already in the office, and he was crying. The wife of one of the neighbors told us (I remember the exact phrase in Polish), "A great misfortune awaits you at home." That is all she said, but I realized that something had happened to my father. That morning, he had wanted to kiss us good-bye, and I noticed that when his lips touched my cheek he did not open his eyes. Bronek and I started to cry, but it was when we got home that we found out that our father was dead.

Our mother was devastated. My father had sent her out to shop and to get a little bell repaired that he could use to call her. He died during her absence, from a second heart attack. I remember the next few days as a nightmare. The weather was absolutely dreadful: wet snow and wind. Many of our relatives came to Grajewo to attend the funeral. All I remember about the funeral is a very long service in the church and a long ceremony at the cemetery in the bitter cold.

Afterward Bronek and I went to Laski, and at the end of the 1937–38 school year I went to live with Janina and her family. Later, I spent some time with my aunt Anna Matuszewska. According to a financial arrangement unknown to me at the time, every month I spent with the Matuszewskis a certain amount, in dollars, was subtracted from the debt that family owed to my mother from the sale of the family estate. I went through the sixth grade being coached by Janina, Dzidka, and others.

At the beginning of 1938, I passed my entrance examination for Stefan Żeromski High School in Warsaw. I was very proud of my uniform (it was the same for all the high schools in Poland), which was navy blue with thin light blue stripes. Those colors signified the first four years of high school (*gimnazjum*); maroon stripes designated the last two years (*lyceum*). On my left sleeve I wore a shield, also light blue, with the number of my school: 96. Throughout the 1938–39 school year I lived with my paternal grandmother, Helena. She tried to be nice to me, but we really did not get along. At least once a week we dined with one of her daughters, Hania or Stasia—not pleasant occasions for me.

The Żeromski *gimnazjum* and *lyceum* was a private institution with an intellectual and politically liberal staff, some of whom were

Jewish, and a high percentage of Jewish students. It was there that I got to know personally many Jewish boys, and I became friendly with several of them. They belonged to upper-class, highly assimilated professional families. The director of the school, Teofil Wojeński, a good friend of Janina's, was a well-known educator, a man of the non-Communist left. He survived the war and played a role in the reconstruction of education in postwar Poland, at least at the beginning of the Communist regime.

I remember a very energetic and extremely leftist geography teacher. Like many leftists in Poland, she was not at all pro-Soviet. "Tam rządzi podła tyrania" (An abominable tyranny rules there), she used to say. She led us on topographical excursions and taught us how to read military maps. I also remember an enormously fat French teacher, Madame Opulski, who liked good-looking boys— therefore, not me—but she was an excellent language teacher, and she taught me a lot of French grammar. After hearing a lot of French in our family and receiving frequent interventions and corrections (*en français, bien entendu*) from Dzidka, I was well prepared for the formal study of that language.

I spent the last summer vacation before the war in Warka. By then my mother had recovered from the shock of her husband's death, and we spent a great deal of time together. Each of us children considered himself or herself her favorite. She continued her informal social work, this time among younger Jewish women. She helped them find access to medical care and solve many other bureaucratic problems.

I believe that my mother chose to work among the Jewish women because they were even less integrated into the life of our small Polish town than men. Her particular friend, and a contact to other women, was a young woman named Hava (Eve). During the war, in the summer of 1941, I told Hava's father that my mother had been arrested. He answered immediately, "What a pity, she was a good woman, so good that she could have been a Jewess." I understood well that this was the highest compliment he could think of.

THREE

The War Years

On Friday, September 1, 1939, I found myself still in Warka. In the morning, at about ten o'clock, I was playing soccer in the meadows close to the Pilica River. Suddenly about twenty planes flew overhead and dropped what looked like packages of leaflets. One of my older friends, who knew everything, explained to us that the planes were the new models of the Polish air force and that we had only thirty of them. No sooner had he spoken than some of the "leaflets" exploded. But not all of them. Later, we found several unexploded bombs with an inscription in Czech. The Germans had taken them after the subjugation of Czechoslovakia. As soon as we heard the explosions, we ran into town, where we learned that the war had begun. A few minutes later a bomb exploded nearby. I ran into the closest house and encountered a tall old Jew wearing a prayer shawl. He did not say anything to me. I realized later that it was one of the rare times that I was inside a Jewish home.

The war brought immediate shortages. Our mother, being absolutely honest, did not keep any tobacco or cigarettes for herself but sold everything. I know that we could have lived comfortably for several months if we had kept some cigarettes hidden, as they became terribly expensive. Everything disappeared from the stores. There was no electricity. My mother found a young couple who had a radio that ran on batteries, which she used to organize a local information service. Every morning she listened to the news, wrote it down, and passed it on to the people who went to Mass. Practically all her life, my mother attended daily Mass, usually taking one of us with her. This information service continued approximately until the final collapse of the Polish army.

The Germans entered Warka on about September 7. My reaction was physical. I had a high fever and stayed in bed for about twenty-four hours. At first, the Germans behaved quite well. Although they demanded the immediate handing over of radios and weapons, a young and, I remember, handsome officer gave my mother a paper saying that she could keep her husband's saber as a souvenir. The saber hung on the wall as decoration. Later, we rarely if ever encountered such manifestations of chivalry. On September 17 the Soviet army, German allies, entered eastern Poland. Warsaw fell at the end of September, and the last Polish troops surrendered on October 2.

The first months of the occupation were characterized by a return to the preindustrial era. The Germans removed all goods, and people rediscovered such old artisan crafts as rope making. The lack of electricity created a black market: German soldiers sold diesel fluid (used instead of coal oil for lamps) for butter: one liter of diesel for one pound of butter.

Suddenly those who declared themselves ethnic Germans (*Volksdeutsche*) became very powerful. One *Volksdeutsch* woman began to make menacing remarks about my mother. It was time to leave Warka. There was no postal service and no transportation of any kind except for horse-driven wagons. My mother wrote a letter to a friend, a landowner, asking him to send a team of horses and a wagon because we had to leave Warka and go to Brzeźce, my mother's birthplace. The letter was carried by a smart young boy. A day or two later, a cart driven by two fine horses appeared. The driver was an old man who remembered my mother as the young daughter of the proprietor of the estate. He kissed her hand and addressed her as *panienka* (little young lady).

The next day, my mother and the five of us children, plus Wiktoria, who was still with us, started our sad voyage, taking with us only the most essential clothes and bedding. It was one of those terribly cold and rainy November days. What stuck in my mind was the picture of a somber Małgosia trying to keep warm under her soggy cotton quilt. We arrived at the Brzeźce estate in the evening. I have already written about the reception at my mother's first cousin's home. It was very sad.

I soon made friends at neighboring Szczyty, the estate of my mother's other cousin. It was proposed that I would live there and assume the function of an undershepherd. I helped the old shepherd (who, I was sure, was a bit of a wizard). I fed the sheep, cleaned their stable, and as soon as spring came guarded the forty-five grazing sheep. The old shepherd lent me his very smart dog, and thus until the fall of 1940 I led the ordinary life of a medieval youth.

I shall always remember with gratitude the reception of Michał and Lucyna Bagniewski, as well as their two sons. They treated me kindly and even paid me for my work in the common currency of the early war: pork fat (*słonina*). I remember how proud I was to give my mother a kilo of pork fat. That was a real treasure, because my mother, Bronek, and Franek were living in an old lumber room or storehouse and had only meager food rations. Franek showed me how to prepare potatoes without any fat (you "fry" them in hot water).

The beginning of the war in Poland was characterized by incredible optimism. Everybody believed France, with Great Britain's assistance, would soon defeat Hitler. A common saying was, "As the sun rises higher [in the spring], Sikorski [chief of the Polish government in France] comes closer to Poland." Only the defeat of France in the summer of 1940 brought the Poles to their senses.

By that time everybody knew about the spontaneous growth of various *konspiracja* organizations and the presence of various groups of "forest boys." Throughout the German occupation, the fundamental optimism of the Polish population was translated into thousands of jokes to support the spirit of resistance and maintain the hope of liberation. I will quote only one, which is linguistically clever. During the defeat of Mussolini and his deposition by the king, the Poles started to repeat the message they "received" from him: "Tutto finito, dupę obito, Benito." While the first phrase, "All is lost," is genuinely Italian, the second is Italianized Polish meaning, "(My) backside was beaten," but it rhymes with *finito* and *Benito* and sounds Italian. This kind of resistance humor also flourished in "socialist" Poland after the war.

In the fall of 1940, after having rusticated for a full year, I returned to Janina's Warsaw house. I started to study at my old high school, which by then had become a German-approved school, the Preparatory School for Commerce Personnel. All the Polish high schools, and of course the universities, had been shut down by the Germans. Most of the prewar teachers were at the approved school. However, the Jews, both teachers and students, had disappeared. They had gone to the newly formed ghetto or into hiding. Getting an education, either in clandestine small groups (*komplety*) or in half-legal schools like ours, had become a patriotic duty. Madame Opulski could not teach French because during the war we were forced to study German. But she offered private French lessons, and I was lucky enough to be taught by her for at least three years. She had been trained in St. Petersburg before World War I, and after World War II she switched to teaching Russian.

Of course, the German language became very important. In our school it was taught throughout the war by an actual German. She was quite young. Apparently she had married a Polish officer before the war. Her husband was sent to the officers' POW camp (*Oflag*), and she refused to divorce him, which, according to German racial laws, she was required to do. Instead, she went into hiding among the Polish population. She acquired a false Polish name that she could barely pronouce. We never discussed such things with her because of the rules of *konspiracja*, but we knew that she was German. Three seconds of listening to her Polish would convince anyone of that fact. She must have been trusted by her Polish colleagues, though, because she knew that under the pretext of learning "commercial" subjects we were, in fact, following the prewar high school curriculum as closely as possible. Thus Polish language and literature was called commercial correspondence, chemistry became *Warenkunde* (science of materials), mathematics was bookkeeping, and so on.

I remember that sometime in about 1942 the German police were rounding up civilians on the streets, checking their papers and arresting suspicious persons. There was a lot of shouting and roaring of trucks and an occasional shot or two. We were on the third floor of a big building on Marszałkowska Street. The German teacher said to us in her colorful Polish, "You must remember, my boys, that what you see and hear is not the real Germany." I am sure that she was right, but this was difficult to believe in 1942.

But what I remember most from Żeromski High School before and during the war was my teacher of Polish language and literature, Marian Wichrzycki. We called him "Wicher" (Strong Wind). He was a nontraditional and inspired teacher. He died in the Uprising as a company commander, fighting under the pseudonym "Sword" (Miecz) in the same regiment that I was in (Baszta). Apparently he had been a Communist in his youth, and as a former Communist he was totally distrustful of Stalin. A few days before the Uprising, I met him on the street. He told me that the Uprising would be successful only if it started when the Russians were already on the western edge of Warsaw.

His mistrust of Stalin was a minority opinion among us. He was, alas, right. I regret very much that I did not encounter him during the fighting. I was told by the members of his company that he carried dozens of photographs of his former students in his pocket. There is no doubt in my mind that after my mother and Janina, Wicher was the greatest influence in my life. He was a devoted teacher and a real friend. He made me want to become a teacher.

During the war, Kazimierz and Janina Dembowski became very poor; they lived on the meager income from their illegal teaching. I realize what a great hardship my presence must have been to them. In addition to their two grown-up daughters, Anna and Jadwiga, and me, they had two paying boarders. One was a distant nephew of Janina's named Stanisław Eustachiewicz, who apparently emigrated to Australia after the war. The other was a young and brilliant fellow who shared our big room. He had a distinctly Jewish name, Zylberberg, but non-Jewish identity papers. We all knew that he was at least half Jewish. Stanisław too was Jewish according to the Nazi laws.

I tried to help Janina's household financially by bringing home white bread from an illegal bakery on the outskirts of Warsaw. It was illegal because the Germans made the use of wheat flour *verboten* for the non-German population. These trips by tram early in the morning were fatiguing. The sale of the illegal bread to friends who were better off brought a little profit to Janina's family. My first year in Warsaw was very difficult because of the lack of food. I was very hungry most of the time.

But the next school year my situation improved. After the start of the German-Soviet war, the German authorities paid less attention to the black market. Furthermore, I was accepted at the famous Orphanage, where Franek had been accepted a year before. Both of us were accepted because the RGO authorities considered us orphans. To be declared an orphan, one's parents had to be dead, imprisoned, or expelled by the Germans from their residence that was now incorporated into the Reich.

The horrible year 1942–43 saw the destruction of the Polish Jews. We knew what was happening to the Jews, and we were sure that if Germany won the war, we would be next. In my circles, even former anti-Semites were terrified by the fate of the Jews and scared for their own future. The destruction of the Warsaw Jews took place in the late summer of 1942.

In retrospect, the Bursa was an island of relative peace in the stormy atmosphere of occupied Warsaw. All of us knew that one of our tutors was a Jew in hiding. We boys occupied the third floor, and the girls' section was on the fifth. We studied like mad and socialized during organized patriotic and theatrical evenings. We also sang in a choir led by a beautiful young woman who arrived just before the curfew and taught us to sing. She spent the night in our small infirmary room. Our fellows fought to make up her room after she had spent the night. I remember that one of them insisted that her pillow smelled divinely.

I realized very soon that many of the older orphans were in fact in *konspiracja*. We slept on three-tiered bunkbeds in two or three big dormitories. One of the older fellows was famous for talking in his sleep. He constantly gave loud, evidently military commands until somebody woke him up. I learned later that he was in the noncommissioned officers' training program, and he obviously took his training deeply to heart.

IN *KONSPIRACJA*

After about a month or so in the Bursa I was approached by two boys a bit older than me. Mieczysław (Mietek) Chorąży and Jerzy (Jurek) Kłoczowski started to talk about my joining a clandestine organization, the ZWZ (Związek Walki Zbrojnej, or Union for Armed Combat), also called PZP (Polskie Związki Powstańcze, or Polish Insurrectional Unions). But already people like Kłoczowski were using the name Armia Krajowa (AK), or Homeland Army. I looked terribly young, but according to Mietek and Jurek I was seventeen years old: in Poland and especially in the military one's age was calculated on the basis of the year of one's birth; for example, in 1942 everybody born in the last week of 1925, including me, was seventeen. I agreed to join immediately, and very soon I was sworn in.

The swearing-in ceremony was brief but moving. It stressed our obedience to the president and government of Poland (in exile in London) and was reinforced by a solemn and powerful religious oath. It was presided over by the platoon leader, whose real name, I learned later, was Karol Niewiarowski. He had an English pseudonym, "Starter." He was certainly old, at least twenty-five. If I remember correctly, he was a sublieutenant. He died in the first hours of the Uprising. Kłoczowski, "Piotruś," my squad leader, and Mieczysław Chorąży, "Grom I," his second in command, were the only other people present. Both Kłoczowski and Chorąży, although wounded, survived the war. Both became outstanding scholars in Poland, Kłoczowski a historian, Chorąży a cancer specialist.

Before the swearing-in ceremony, I was asked to choose a pseudonym. I told them that I wanted to be "Syn," Polish for "son." I wanted to honor my mother, who was already dead (although we did not want to believe it). The mind-set of many of the youths in the AK was antisentimental and antiemotional, so later I told my colleagues that I had said "Sym" but that Starter had misunderstood me. (Igo Sym was the name of a notorious actor who became a *Volksdeutsch* and was executed by the *konspiracja* early in the occupation. It would have been absolutely insane for a Polish patriot like me to take his name as a pseudonym.)

I was told later that our unit was called Baszta (Turret), but in fact the term was a combination of *BA*talion *SZTA*bowy (Headquarters Defense Battalion). Apparently its organization dated to 1939. I spent all my service in that battalion, which later became the Baszta Regiment. We went through the standard infantry training of the pre-1939 army. We were trained in small groups, never more than six in one room. We studied basic army customs and language. I remember that in our outfit we did not use the term "Sir" (*pan*) in addressing a superior but rather "Citizen" (*obywatel*). This custom stemmed from the early days of Baszta, whose organizers were men of the political (but not Communist) left. I believe that the use of *obywatel* continued until the Uprising.

We chiefly studied basic Polish and German arms: rifles, pistols, machine pistols, and machine guns. Later, we also learned how to use British weapons dropped by parachute. We met in various apartments, the addresses of which were always given in a sort of cipher. You added, say, 3 to the number of the house and 4 to the number of the apartment: thus Sienkiewicz Street 14, apt. 7, became Sienkiewicz Street 17, apt. 11. The cipher numbers varied from time to time. Our meetings were held late in the afternoon, and we often spent long evenings studying. Since it was well past the curfew, we would crash on the floor of the apartment and leave early in the morning, either alone or accompanied by one other person.

We were usually prudent, and the local friendly civilians, although afraid of the Germans, were on our side. I remember two incidents that demonstrate the atmosphere of the time. During a small-arms demonstration, one of the trainees inadvertently fired a bullet, which went through the wall into the neighboring apartment. Fortunately, nobody was hit. The fellows left the apartment quietly and in an orderly fashion, but one person stayed behind and covered the hole on our side with plaster. We did not meet there again (we always called such an apartment a "local"), but the owners of the "local" told us later that the neighbors never inquired about the hole in their wall.

I also heard that on one occasion one of us went to the wrong apartment. A man opened the door and listened to the identifying password, "I came for the carbide lamp." He answered, "You came to the wrong apartment, the carbide lamp boys meet on the floor below." I do not know whether this story is true, but it illustrates the fact that a *konspiracja* on such a large scale—on August 1, 1944, about forty thousand insurgents began the Uprising—could not exist without the friendly collaboration of the public at large.

After several weeks of basic training (about three times a week), I was considered ready for the noncommissioned officers' training course. The idea was that the Baszta, if possible, was to be a cadre unit. In other words, everybody was trained as either a noncommissioned officer or an officer. Kłoczowski and Chorąży had graduated from the officers' training course, but I was too young. I received my German identity card (*Kennkarte*) a few days before my swearing-in ceremony. It somehow survived the war. That I looked so young, which I was very ashamed of at the time, would serve me well later, when I was arrested by the Gestapo.

I finished the course successfully. As I mentioned earlier, we were trained as a small unit, meeting in different apartments. We were taught weapons handling and sharpshooting. There was an ingenious little instrument, an imitation of a gunsight, fixed on the table. The trainee looked at the wall, on which was affixed a piece of cardboard with a dot on it. The trainee told the instructor to move the dot until it represented an accurate aim. We became quite good shots, a skill that would soon be tested in the Uprising.

Toward the end of the course we used a training table: a small, three-dimensional table representing a realistic landscape. The instructor told us where our position was and where the enemy position was. He announced that our side was beginning the attack. The trainee's assignment was not to explain the situation but to give immediate orders to his squad. Once, I remember, the instructor described the position as being so desperate for our side that the candidate could only *do modlitwy*, "prepare to pray." Indeed, in the Polish military tradition, the unit gathers in the morning and in the evening, and at the order "*do modlitwy*" the unit sings an appropriate morning or evening religious hymn. The training leader told us that he well understood the hopelessness of the situation he had described and that in this case "prepare to pray" was the correct order.

From time to time we trained in small units in the forest near Warsaw. Training consisted chiefly of simulated infantry attacks on designated enemy positions. We came to the forest and left it individually or in pairs, never in larger groups. I remember one Sunday afternoon, two separate pairs got on the suburban tram very tired and hot. The other passengers looked at us sympathetically. They obviously guessed that we were returning from military exercises, but of course there was no talk about it. *Konspiracja!*

In July 1943 I passed an examination consisting chiefly of landscape table exercises in command, and I became a lance corporal (*strszy strzelec*). I was very proud of this promotion, more proud than of all the other promotions that I have received in my life.

Now my chief role in the organization was as a "runner." Every morning I went to a certain local in the southern part of Warsaw. This apartment was inhabited by four former Bursa members, including Kłoczowski. I picked up messages given orally or, less frequently, written on cigarette paper (in case of trouble the cigarette paper was to be swallowed). Traveling by tram, I delivered the messages to the second in command of our platoon, Cygan. In the prison camp, I learned his wartime name: Stanisław Falkowski. He lived in the northernmost part of Warsaw (Marymont).

Cygan (Gypsy) was a very handsome man and quite dark, like an actual Gypsy. During the Uprising we realized that he loved, and was loved by, all women. One of the women in our city district gave him a full Polish uniform and helmet that had belonged to her husband. He looked splendid in this officer's uniform. After our unsuccessful passage to the city center through the sewers, he was photographed by our German captors, who thought he was a real soldier. During my early morning visits, I realized that he was a Jew in hiding with false papers. Only after the war did he reveal to my former colleagues his Jewish name and background.

Cygan became my platoon leader on the first day of the Uprising, when Starter was killed. After a short time, he received another command and was replaced by Lucjan Sikorski, "Gard." Gard was very musical and played the piano well. He composed the rather catchy tune of the Company B1 song. He was wounded in the right palm, which certainly ended his pianist career. After a short stay in the hospital, Gard came back to his command, one of the walking wounded. He stayed with us until the end of the Uprising. I spent my time in the Stalag with both Cygan and Gard.

Sometime in the fall of 1943 our whole company took part in a large military exercise. We gathered in the forest north of Warsaw on a Sunday morning. If I remember correctly, we were some 150 men. Only a few of us were armed. Those who were armed would protect us, or at least fire warning shots, in case the Germans came too close. Later we realized that the Germans were not willing to enter the forest except in large formations. I believe that our military exercises, dangerous as they were, were intended to raise our morale, and in this they certainly succeeded. We came in small groups from all directions to the designated meeting place. Each group was given exact routes to and from the exercise ground.

The chief exercise was a typical infantry attack and defense. I remember that our armed "protectors" got so excited that during the "attack" they fired some shots in the air. They received a terrible tongue-lashing from the company commander. In the spirit of *konspiracja* we were full of enthusiasm and the desire to fight. After this short exercise and one or two patriotic speeches, there was a field Mass, short but very pious and patriotic. We dispersed quietly and went by our different routes back to town.

One morning early in 1944, I went to the local to pick up the message, but I found an unusual situation. Somebody outside the apartment building told me that everybody in our local had been shot by Germans, who had come on foot and shouted in German to the house porter to open the apartment door. They shot three men, all former students in the Bursa. Only Kłoczowski was not shot; he had gone to visit his parents the day before. One thing was clear to me: the killers were not the Gestapo. The Gestapo never walked; they drove Mercedes. And unless they encountered fire, they would not shoot people without interrogating them first. One possible explanation was that the shooters were Communists. One of our colleagues, "Król," a man of good peasant stock, had apparently joined the Communist AL (People's Army) and then changed his mind and joined our group. Perhaps because he was a "turncoat" he and his apartment fellows were "executed."

I reported the whole affair to Cygan, who passed on the information. The local had to be declared off-limits, since as a rule the Gestapo would wait in the apartment and arrest anyone who entered. Because no police had remained at the local, I believe it was the Communists who had carried out the killing, but I do not know if the incident was ever fully explained.

THE GESTAPO

After being removed from the Bursa in the summer of 1943, I lived with Wanda Gawecka in the apartment where Małgosia had been arrested. Wanda, my mother's second cousin, was a shy, elderly, single woman who was very fond of me because I used to visit her ill mother before the war. Like many other people in Warsaw, she doubtless suspected my *konspiracja* activities, but we never talked about it.

The apartment complex on Karpiński Street consisted of, I think, three or four separate blocks. Our apartment was on the first floor of a smaller block consisting of ten apartments. In the basement, used for storage, there was a large common area and the doors to ten individual compartments, one for each apartment. The individual compartments (storage for coal, potatoes, etc.) were locked. The common area was always open. In one corner some junk was piled up.

On April 6, 1944, I received a telephone call from Grom, my squad leader. He told me that he was in our part of town, and he had to come over at once. He arrived carrying a heavy bag. He told me that the Germans were stopping traffic and checking identity papers between Żolibórz and the city center. It was imprudent to try to get through to the other side of Warsaw, so he had decided to leave the bag with me and proceed home without it. He said that he would pick it up early the next day.

Grom showed me the contents of the bag: one British submachine gun, a Sten; one 45mm Colt revolver; two hand grenades made in Warsaw (*filipinki*); and ammunition. Later I learned that this was part of the gradual transfer of our arms from the bigger secret stores to the place close to our position in the planned Uprising. The Sten gun and the grenades were heavily greased (to protect them from rust) and therefore not immediately usable. Only the Colt was ready to be used.

I put the bag under my bed and said good-bye to Grom. My bed was a day couch, a box with a mattress on it that could be lifted up and bedding stored underneath. Grom was in a hurry because the curfew was approaching, and he left almost immediately. Naturally, I did not say anything to Wanda when she arrived a bit later.

I did not get undressed, and I did not make up my bed. Instead I tried to sleep on the couch, with the Colt tucked in my belt. I was full of premonitions and fears. And sure enough, I was right. At about six o'clock in the morning, I was abruptly awakened by terrible cries and shouts (noises that during the war only Germans were capable of making). Through the window, I saw several Wehrmacht soldiers, fully armed and wearing helmets. I rushed to the common basement and put the bag under the pile of junk. I hesitated about what to do with my Colt. My first thought was to kill myself. In spite of our Christian ideology, we did not consider suicide a religious transgression when faced with the Gestapo.

But I distinctly remember another reason for not blowing my head off: my youthful preoccupation with reputation, the medieval idea of *fama*. What would my colleagues in the AK say if I killed myself "prematurely," without a "valid reason"? After a brief but painful hesitation, I put the Colt in the bag, covered it with the trash, and went up to the first floor.

At the door I saw a German, a Wehrmacht soldier, about thirty-five years old, who obviously saw me coming out of the basement. He did not shout but told me (I still remember the sound of his voice), "Alle Türe aufmachen und Keller auch" (Open all the doors as well as the basement). I said, "Der Keller is immer aufgemacht" (The basement door is always open). He did not answer.

Later we learned that on this day, Good Friday, April 7, 1944, there was a large German police action. It was led by the Gestapo, or more correctly, the Sicherheitsdienst der Waffen SS (Security Service of the SS). The Wehrmacht was used as a support force. It was obvious to most of us that the Wehrmacht soldiers did not enjoy their police role. The German action extended to several blocks of that part of Żolibórz and consisted of inspecting documents and conducting general searches. All the people living in our blocks of apartments were gathered in the inner courtyard while the Germans first checked our *Kennkarten* and then searched our apartments. I was quite happy that I had decided to part with my Colt and began to hope that maybe everything would end well.

Suddenly, at about ten o'clock, I heard the most horrible cries coming from inside our block: "Englische Waffen! Englische Waffen!" (English weapons! English weapons!). There is no doubt in my mind that this was the worst moment of my life. Today, some seventy years after the event, I again feel the horrible emptiness in my stomach. I have to stop writing for a moment . . .

I saw the Gestapo officer running with the Sten in his hand. Some time later, two things happened. First, the Wehrmacht soldier who had seen me coming out of the basement early that morning approached and looked at me persistently, without saying a word. I knew that one word from him to the Gestapo, and I would be dead. He certainly saved my life. The Germans also found in the bag a book with the Polish title *On the Tracks*, by Jack London, supposedly published in 1936, but after three pages of text the book turned out to be a manual on railroad sabotage and the destruction of tracks with explosives, with illustrations. I remembered that I had made some handwritten corrections and notes in the book. Furthermore, the front of my shirt was dirty from the Colt's greasy residue.

The second incident that I remember was this. An older gentleman who lived on the floor above Wanda was standing next to me. I vaguely remembered seeing him. He whispered to me that the person who put the weapons in the common basement should confess to exculpate the others. He must have guessed that I was the guilty person. I, of course, agreed with him. "Yes, you're right, he should confess," I whispered several times, trying to indicate that I was not involved.

After a long wait we were taken in open trucks to Pawiak prison. "We" included all the men and women who lived in our block and all the men from the whole apartment complex, some hundred people in all. My first reaction was a certain satisfaction at being lost in the crowd.

When we arrived at Pawiak—we had to go to the middle of the already demolished Ghetto to get there—we were put in the yard outside the office. The window opened, and a German shouted to the officer in charge, "Keep only 10 percent of this shit and let the others go!" As I would soon learn, there were already too many prisoners in the building. A couple of policemen opened the gate, and they let many people go, without any visible plan. One of the first people released was Wanda, who turned to me and said, "The same thing will happen to you as to Małgosia!" Later, after my release, she denied that she had uttered those words. To prove her faith in my eventual release, she bought a piece of light gray woolen material, from which I had a military-style jacket made in order to be ready for the Uprising.

There was a moment when I might have found myself among those who were released, but one of the policemen kept me back. About twelve of us were detained, including the older gentleman who had wanted me to confess and a young woman from our block. I did not know the other men; they were from other blocks. We entered the office and waited to be registered. I kept my overcoat in my hand and stood straight, like a good boy, but one of the fellows leaned on the counter between us and the policemen. A big SS man beat him enthusiastically with a heavy whip, which every German in Pawiak carried with him. I got the impression that many policemen simply enjoyed beating people.

After registration (name, address, date and place of birth, parents' names, profession, etc.) our group was divided up and sent to different temporary cells. In my temporary cell there was a group of about eight Jews who had been caught without proper documents during that morning's Żolibórz action. One of them, a civilized and sad old man, told me that he and the others did not go through the prison registration process because as Jews they were to be shot. He was very calm, very resigned, and, above all, very tired. In the afternoon an armed SS man took them away. I still remember the face of that Jewish gentleman.

We were taken to a big room, stripped, and searched. The searches, like most duties in Pawiak, were carried out by Ukrainian auxiliaries, and some of them from western Ukraine understood Polish well. I was afraid that they would report that I was wearing German military underwear and socks, but they did not pay attention to it. (Starting in about the summer of 1943, more and more German underclothes were sold by the soldiers, usually the eastern "volunteers." One could buy them at the popular flea market in Kerceli Square.) Very soon our heads were shaved and our clothes returned, minus money and valuables.

After a long wait, we were taken to one of the basement cells that served as "quarantine" areas. We spent from ten to fourteen days there. The cells were terribly crowded and dirty, with scarcely enough room to sleep on the floor. In the daytime, half of us stood up so the other half could sit. After a few days, we looked like the proverbial *Untermenschen* (subhumans), dirty, scared, and stinking. Because the basement cell was so overcrowded, it was stiflingly hot. I remember that we were displayed to groups of young SS men who were sent on excursions to Pawiak, as if we were animals in a zoo. They were supposed to get to know "the face of the enemy." How many of them would soon rot in Soviet camps!

A bucket in the corner served as our toilet. Defecation was discouraged by the cell bullies, who either were or pretended to be criminals. Every morning we were run to the washroom, but there was scarcely any time to defecate. The guards shouted "Schnell! Schnell!" (Hurry! Hurry!) and beat those who were on the pot to speed up the process. Some of the men, however, managed even to wash their hands and faces. Older prisoners suffered much more from that haste than young fellows like me.

In the evening of the first day we received some soup and bread. I soon learned that the food was rough but in sufficient quantity. The horrible hunger in Pawiak in the years 1940–43 had ended when some of the high SS administrators were captured and executed by the AK. Their successors got the point, and the food improved in quantity. They also allowed the RGO to give us additional food, and our families were permitted to send individual parcels to us. I got one parcel from Janina during my stay in Pawiak. I learned much later that our underground authorities had demanded all these "privileges" from the German administrators under the threat of execution. The food was often pea soup, with many little (well-cooked) worms floating on the surface. The advice given by the older prisoners was, "Close your eyes and eat it."

Under the Ukrainian guards were prisoner trustees. Each cell had a *Zellälteste* (cell elder). His main duties were to shout "Achtung!" when a guard opened the door and, once a day, during the *Appell*, report to the German guard. (The Ukrainians were unworthy of receiving a report.) I was so impressed with the *Appell* that to this day I remember the formula used by the *Zellälteste*: "Herr Scharführer, ich melde gehorsamst Zelle zweihundert sieben und fünfzig belegt mit acht und dreizig Häftlige, alle anwesend, gesund, und zufrieden" (Sir, I report most obediently, cell number 257, occupied by 38 prisoners. All present, healthy, and satisfied). This last adjective was certainly proof that the Germans had a sense of humor.

Each block had a prisoner *Schreiber* (scribe). His job was to keep the list of prisoners in a given cell and a list of those who were sent to Gestapo headquarters, to the hospital, and so on. The *Schreiber* of our block was a nice young Jewish intellectual. The Germans had probably installed him on the divide-and-conquer principle, hoping that we would become anti-Semitic. But his appointment was a mistake: he was very astute and managed to carry out the Germans' orders, shouting and kicking us when they were around, but he quietly encouraged us when we were alone.

Life in our cell was very hard, but harder still were my fears concerning the interrogations at Gestapo headquarters, which was housed in the former Polish Ministry of Education on Szuh Avenue (Aleja Szuha). I was absolutely convinced that any reasonably good policeman would figure out that I was the person who had hidden the arms in the common basement. I was the only young man living in our apartment block, and along with the weapons, I had left my textbook on train sabotage, in which I had written notes. Besides that, the old gentleman could share his opinions about me with the Gestapo. I was so tired that Good Friday night that, squeezed between two prisoners, I fell asleep immediately, but I also remember that I woke up early, absolutely terrified when I realized that I was in the dreadful Pawiak.

The next day was Holy Saturday. Because of the coming of Easter we received some extra food sent by the RGO, and that morning people in our cell were singing the Polish Easter hymn, "Wesoły nam dzień dziś nastał" (A Joyful Day Came to Us Today). The stark contrast between our situation and the joyful news of the Resurrected One was, I am sure, not lost on anyone in the cell.

I expected to be taken to Szuh Avenue the next day, but I was wrong. If I remember correctly, I wasn't taken to Gestapo headquarters until at least two weeks later, when I was already in the upper block, which was a little more spacious and cleaner, although invaded by millions of fleas, which lived in our thin straw mattresses (in the basement cells we had slept on the cement floor).

One day several of us were taken in a special "Black Maria" under the heavy guard of fully armed SS men. When we arrived at Szuh Avenue we were put in the basement cell, which was separated from the hall only by an iron grid. The place was called "streetcar" (*tramway*) because the seats faced the nonexistent driver, with their backs facing the hall, which contained the SS guards. Any attempt to look back, or to talk audibly to any prisoner, was immediately met with horrible shouts from the policemen and a severe beating.

In the "streetcar" I saw a very old man. The Germans were bragging that he was the brother of the former Polish president, Mościcki. The old gentleman was completely lost. We, the young fellows, had to whisper to him to guide him around. My memories of the "streetcar" were refreshed a few years ago when I visited Warsaw. This part of the surviving ministry building is now a small museum.

I also remember a young fellow who was brought back to the "streetcar" after interrogation, severely beaten. He was completely broken, and he wanted to speak, or rather whisper, to me. He told me that he was a member of the NSZ (Narodowe Siły Zbrojne, National Armed Forces), a right-wing *konspiracja* group not co-ordinated with the AK, and was caught red-handed. He was desperate; he had abandoned all the rules of the *konspiracja* and even suggested that he had given away all the secrets he knew. He horribly regretted being involved with the *konspiracja*. His state terrified me further.

Finally I heard my name called, and I met my interrogator, a big blond, obviously an Austrian. (Most of the Security Services people of the SS in Poland were from Austria; apparently Himmler believed that the Austrians were better able to resist Slavic charm than their German colleagues.) The interrogator took me to his office, on the fourth floor, I believe, and at the entrance hit me several times with his whip. I cried out, according to the rules of behavior that I had learned in my training. He asked me if I spoke German. I answered with feigned enthusiasm, "Ich spreche sehr gut" (I speak very well), with such un-German pronunciation that he immediately called in a *Dolmetscher* (interpreter). Again, I was following the *konspiracja* instructions about being arrested: be nice and "helpful," and remember that an interpreter gives you more time to think about your answers.

It was a warm day at the end of April; the window in the office was open. It occurred to me that if things became difficult, I could perhaps jump out the window. We waited several minutes. I was standing at attention, covered in sweat. The interrogator was reading official papers in front of him, glancing threateningly at me from time to time. He was smoking a cigarette in a long glass cigarette holder.

Suddenly, his cigarette fell out of the holder. Ever so polite, in an appropriately subservient manner, I asked, "Kann ich die Zigarette aufnehmen?" (May I pick up the cigarette?). He looked at me like a lord and master, proud of his position and of the fact that I obviously understood this position. He acquiesced with a nod, and I came closer, picked up his cigarette, and put it on the desk. While doing so I eagerly glanced at the document he was reading. Judging from the addresses mentioned in it, he was not reading my case but something unconnected with me. I was immediately filled with enormous but concealed relief.

Finally, a female translator stepped in. She was a young and slutty-looking *Volksdeutsch*, heavily made up. She did not even glance at me, but she began to flirt with my interrogator. She told him that the *Kriminalpolizei* (Criminal Police) had recovered some of the goods stolen from her.

The interrogation started by establishing my identity (*Grundsätze*): place of birth, name of my father, and when and where he died. I answered, "In 1937 in Grajewo." "Point out the town on the map," he said. I did. I believe that I hesitated a bit about my mother. For a while I wanted to say "Janina," but this was dangerous because of her Jewish background. I am quite sure that I said Henryka, though this was equally dangerous because of her imprisonment at Ravensbrück. (My first hours of imprisonment had completely convinced me that she was no longer alive.)

The policeman asked me where she was. I answered, "She went to work for the German Reich." Again I was following our instructions about imprisonment: tell as much truth as you can. To this day I thank God for sending me an interrogator who was not eager to follow police procedures. He could have checked the name Henryka Dembowska in the huge card index on the first floor, whose existence I had heard about from experienced prisoners. Luckily for me, he did not bother to do it. If he had, I would have been dead.

By 1944 all the next of kin of the executed were routinely killed or sent to a camp.

My interrogator finally asked me a few general questions about the morning of April 7, and then the basic one, "Did you see anybody leaving your apartment block early in the morning?" I swore by the Holy Mother of Częstochowa that I had not seen anybody that morning before the arrival of the German police. That was the only real question in my case. Now I understood that because I looked so young, the policemen who rounded us up didn't think I could be responsible for hiding the weapons. Had I looked like a *stolze Pole* (proud Pole), he would have guessed the truth without any difficulty.

I remember that I was sweating profusely when I signed the interrogation record. But I felt enormous relief. The record did not contain anything that could be technically incriminating. Very soon the interpreter left us, and the interrogator made a sign that we were going down to the "streetcar." While in the office, turning to go out, I looked behind me and saw on the shelf the bag with the compromising book sticking out of it.

Coming back to the "streetcar," I realized that all the other prisoners were pleased to see me in good shape and in a good mood. I was indeed very happy, but I tried to look indifferent. I expected to be sent to a camp, but in my view at the time, the camp was better than waiting to be interrogated.

The group of prisoners with whom I went to Pawiak were all relieved to be leaving the horrible Szuh Avenue building. We were talking about "going home," that is, going back to Pawiak. We laughed a little when a peasant among us insisted on calling Aleja Szuha "Aleja Sucha," or Dry Avenue. (The simple country people around Warsaw confused the *s* and *sz* [pronounced *sh*] consonants.) I was sure that the fellow was not really a simple peasant but only pretending to be one: "Aleja Sucha" was too good a joke, and he played the fool even with us.

Life in the regular cell was more bearable. We had a few real criminals, but they did not bully us. By "us," I mean the political prisoners, who, with two exceptions, pretended to have been arrested like me in mass control actions. We insisted individually that we had been arrested "for innocence" (*za niewinność*); in other words, we all claimed to be victims of the German principle of collective responsibility.

The first of the two exceptions was a man about thirty years old who apparently was arrested on the basis of convincing proof of his involvement in *konspiracja*. He was interrogated at length and badly beaten. He told us that he had signed a "very bad" interrogation record and expected to be shot soon. He talked freely about his involvement with the AK, but we did not respond in kind. I thought, or suspected, that he might be a provocateur. The other "free talker" was a little Frenchman who was sent to a German factory in Poland as a "voluntary" worker. He was a simple chap who knew very little German and no Polish. He was happy when he discovered that I spoke French. He told me that his prospects were bad because he had committed *"un petit sabotage."*

Life in Pawiak consisted of waiting, waiting to be called to be transported to a concentration camp or to Szuh Avenue. Some prisoners were taken away early in the morning to be executed. We all knew the subtle aspects of the procedure: the names of those who were to be executed were called out in the morning without shouting and without explanation; those going to the Gestapo were called more roughly, and often police headquarters was mentioned. In April and May 1944 many executions were carried out in the territory of the destroyed Ghetto. I remember at least one occasion when one of our cellmates was taken to be shot. We would wait for those who were returning from Szuh Avenue. We tried to help the men who had been badly beaten, but moral support was all that we could offer. During the quick weekly shower I saw some severely beaten prisoners. During the *Appell* we had to report some of them as *krank* (sick).

We spent our time worrying about our future but not talking about it. To kill time, some of the prisoners played (homemade) cards, talking quietly about unimportant things, waiting for the soup, and yearning to smoke tobacco. Tobacco was absolutely forbidden by the prison authorities. Occasionally some tobacco came in a food parcel from home or as a gift from an old Polish doctor who was supposed to take care of prisoners but had at his disposal only two remedies: aspirin and vaseline and some cigarettes. (Legend had it that this doctor was one of the first prisoners of German-ruled Pawiak.) Nicotine deprivation was very difficult for prisoners, and it was then that I decided that I would never smoke cigarettes. My conviction was further strengthened by my stay in the Stalag, a prisoner of war camp for soldiers and NCOs. In fact, I have never smoked cigarettes, but as a young professor I pretended to smoke a pipe, to give myself a more "mature" look.

There is one amusing (and completely atypical) thing that I remember from my stay in Pawiak. I did not play cards, but I participated in *dupniak*, the "arse-beating game." One person held down another fellow's head in his lap. The bent-down fellow could not see the group of men behind him. One of them struck a heavy blow with his hand on the victim's backside. After each slap the victim tried to guess who had hit him. If he did not guess, he was hit again until he guessed correctly. Then the striker became in turn the receiver. (It is difficult to look innocent after striking a heavy blow.)

One day during the game, the SS man in charge of our block saw us playing and entered the cell on the sly, without allowing the *Zellälteste* to shout "Achtung!," which would have interrupted us. The SS man apparently adored *dupniak*. The receiver was usually afraid to recognize him, but occasionally he became the receiver. Some of the prisoners decided to play a trick on him. We organized two games played simultaneously. When the SS man became the receiver, he was hit by the receiver of the other team instead of one of the normal participants. We beat the fellow for about five minutes, until someone from the proper team struck him. He was a good player and quickly guessed who had hit him. But I do not believe that he realized our deception.

We called the SS man "Nosek" (Little Nose), because he had lost a part of his nostril. He was a simple but probably decent fellow. His superiors' teaching about the inferiority of the prisoners' races was less important to him than his passion for *dupniak*. This was the only example of a sort of German fraternization with the enemy that I ever encountered in Pawiak, or elsewhere in occupied Poland.

"NICHT WIEDERKOMMEN!"

On the morning of May 3, we were talking about the possibility of executions. It was Polish Constitution Day (a new constitution passed by the parliament in 1792, three years before the final partition of Poland), and we thought that the Gestapo would celebrate by staging a big public execution. Indeed, at about nine o'clock in the morning, Nosek entered the cell, the shout "Achtung!" was heard, and we got up and stood at attention facing him. He called one name: "Dembowski." For a moment I thought that it was my end, but the other prisoners did not look concerned. Nosek was in a good mood, too. He told me to take my things and follow him. I began to feel less afraid because he took me to the inner court and left me with a few other prisoners. They told me that we were being released. Although I was suspicious, I allowed myself to hope.

Suddenly in the yard I saw my first cousin, Andrzej Kwiatkowski, who had been arrested some weeks before. He was very happy to see me and quickly said that he was a trustee working in the prison yard and that he was sure we were being released. The Germans, he said, never left those who were to be executed without a guard. He gave me a message to deliver to his mother.

Another SS man took us to Szuh Avenue. We waited briefly in the "streetcar." A number of SS men shouted, "Nicht wiederkommen!" (Don't come back!), at us. Even these roughneck Austrian policemen seemed happy to see some people set free. In the interrogator's office I was told, without an interpreter, that I was going home. I did not see anybody from the group that had been arrested with me. The bag with the book was still on the shelf. I received a document that I still remember verbatim: it stated that the bearer was being released from the SD (*SD Gefängniss*) prison and that *"die Polizeibehörde sind geboten den Obergenanten frei zu lassen"* (police authorities are asked to let the above-named person go free). It was a priceless document.

I left the Gestapo building alone. It was a warm, sunny day, and I was terribly dirty, holding my heavy overcoat. Szuh Avenue is very close to Słoneczna Street and Janina's apartment. I could be there in a few minutes, but once a *konspirator* always a *konspirator*. I decided to follow procedure and telephone my aunt to make sure that no German police were stationed there. I went into a small store and asked the lady behind the counter if I could use her telephone.

The custom in wartime Warsaw, where there were no public telephones, was to use the telephones in stores and pay according to the accepted tariff. (Incidentally, the Polish formula "May I phone?," "Czy mogę zadzwonić? "Can I ring up?," explains the origin of my brother Franek's strange and certainly antiheroic AK pseudonym, Dzwonek. Devoted to practical jokes, Franek would go into a nice store and ask, "Can I ring up?" If the answer was yes, he would pull a little bell from his pocket, ring it for about ten seconds, and then leave. I am sure that I am the only one who still remembers the secret of his pseudonym.)

The lady in the store immediately understood that I had just come from "over there." Yes, she said, and you do not have to pay. This was fortunate, because I had no money; the few *złotys* that I had brought to Pawiak had been confiscated by the Ukrainians searching my effects. The lady brought me a chair and asked if I had by chance met so-and-so "over there." I told her that there were many people "over there" and that I had not encountered him. I did not tell her that we did not use family names.

I phoned. Anula Dembowska answered. She almost fainted when I told her that I was out. "Come home at once, you old bull [*stary byku*]," she cried. In her language "old bull" was an expression of great affection. I went home. If the Gestapo officer's discovery of the weapons was the worst moment of my life, coming home to the Słoneczna Street was the most joyful one. Janina was home. There was an inexpressible sense of joy, in fact a sense that my liberation was a miracle. Releases from Pawiak were rare.

Anula immediately made a plate of my favorite dish, flour dumplings (*kluski kładzione*) with pork grease. It was afternoon, and I had only eaten a meager breakfast, but I was so excited and had so much to talk about that I hardly ate anything. I told and retold my adventures in Pawiak and at Szuh Avenue, without, of course, mentioning anything about my involvement with the weapons. Hearing of my liberation, many friends came. They wanted to know all about what it was like in prison and being interrogated. Such knowledge could be very important to all of us, and they knew it.

For security reasons I did not return to my aunt Gawecka. Among other things, I was afraid that the old gentleman who suspected me might have been released, too. Janina asked me to stay with them, but I did not want to change my address on my *Kennkarte.* Wanda Gawecka came to see me with the wool material for my jacket and told me an obvious fib: "I always knew that you would be released."

Soon I got in touch with Grom, one of the few members of the *konspiracja* whose address I knew by then. I gave him an exhaustive report about my stay in Pawiak. He took some notes on the usual cigarette paper and told me to stay away from everybody until he told me differently. I was shocked when Grom told me that he had not left his lodgings after my arrest. "We trusted you," he said. But he had not followed the *konspiracja* rule that one should abandon lodgings known to a prisoner of the Gestapo. I knew that my superiors trusted me, but at times like these, routines were routines. Grom told me that I had been promoted to the rank of corporal while I was in Pawiak. With my usual sense of humor, I told him, and later my AK comrades, that the promotion was meant to be posthumous.

The next morning, I went to my school. The joyous reception at Słoneczna Street was repeated there. For every class, every new teacher, I had to repeat everything I had seen and heard on Szuh Avenue and in Pawiak. Marian Wichrzycki was obviously beside himself with joy. My German teacher cried unashamedly over the happy surprise of seeing me alive. Later I told her that I had made great progress in speaking that *"vermaledeite Mundart"* (bloody dialect; i.e., German).

All my colleagues, knowing my legendary appetite, shared their sandwiches with me. But on that day it was difficult to eat. I suspected that their joy was not just personal but political as well. Most of my schoolmates, I suspected, were in *konspiracja*. Although nobody talked about it openly, one could guess the ones who belonged by a certain interest in military subjects, a military way of speaking, and even certain gestures, like heel clicking. I talked to Wichrzycki about the coming final exams and told him that I would study alone and be ready for them at the end of June.

Janina and Kazimierz decided that I should leave Warsaw for a couple of weeks to rest and fatten up—I had lost quite a lot of weight during my imprisonment—and to recover from the strong emotions of recent events. We got in touch with our second cousins on my father's side, Eugenia (Genia) and Stanisław (Staś) Hempel. They owned a little piece of land near Krasnystaw (Lublin district) called Nowiny. I traveled there by train with Anula, an old friend of Genia's.

In Nowiny in May 1944 the atmosphere was quite different from that in Warsaw. Polish partisans from the AK were deeply entrenched. The Germans moved cautiously during the day and stayed put at night. In general, they kept away from small places. Most people thought that the war would be over that summer. In fact, the Soviets entered that part of Poland in July 1944 and formed the Polish Committee of National Liberation, the future Polish Communist government, on July 22.

Genia and Staś received us well. Also living in their house was an old lady—a cousin—and a young and strikingly handsome Sicilian, from the town of Enna, who gave his name as Gaetano Alessandro. After the fall of Mussolini, the young Gaetano had managed to get involved with the German SS. He joined as a foreign member but promptly deserted in the Lublin district, in early 1944, on his way to the eastern front. The *konspiracja* people furnished him with a false *Kennkarte* with a Polish name. Because he spoke only Italian, they had put in the *Kennkarte* that he was deaf and mute. He was very proud of his "handicap." I have no idea what became of Gaetano. When I was in southern Italy a year later, in the summer of 1945, I wrote a letter to the municipality of Enna (again known by its pre-Fascist name, Castrogiovanni) telling them of my encounter with Gaetano Alessandro. I did not receive a response.

After a nice, lazy week at Nowiny, we were visited by two military-looking men. They informed Staś that a detachment of the AK would soon arrive in Nowiny. Indeed, about twenty well-armed men came the next day. They were exhausted and needed rest. As soon as they were settled in the barn, they took off their boots in order to tend to their sore feet. Anula, a medical student, helped them. After a few days they were rested and their feet more or less healed. They wanted to learn how to drive. They sent several men to the highway and stopped the first German truck they saw, confiscating it along with the driver's weapons. The truck was used as a driver's training vehicle until it ran out of gas.

After day or so, a detachment of the German Wehrmacht appeared, marching slowly toward Nowiny. The partisans withdrew to the nearby forest, taking the Italian with them.

Genia, Staś, Anula, and I got into a horse-driven cart and rode away but without haste since the Wehrmacht was approaching slowly, obviously avoiding direct confrontation with the AK. Only the old lady was left in Nowiny. She explained to the German officer that there were no partisans there and that everybody had left because they were afraid of reprisals. The Hempels, Anula, and I went back to the house that evening. This incident was not at all typical of partisan activity, but in the summer of 1944 the Wehrmacht often avoided direct confrontations with the partisans in that district. I left Nowiny with Anula shortly afterward.

Back in Warsaw, I began my usual *konspiracja* activities. When I met with Kłoczowski, I learned that during my imprisonment my squad had had a two-day training exercise in the forest of Kampinos, north of Warsaw. They had met with a small detachment of the Jewish Fighting Organization (ŻOB, Żydowska Organizacja Bojowa). Piotruś showed me photographs of them with our people. My first reaction was childish irritation that life had continued so well without me.

Dzidka came to see me around that time. She told me that her people from the hand grenade factory, who had some contacts in the German Criminal Police, had paid a bribe for my liberation from Pawiak. Much later, after the war, I learned that in 1944 there were indeed a certain number of cases of prisoners who had been arrested without serious evidence of guilt being freed as the result of a generous bribe. Dzidka said that since the sum paid was significant, she wanted me to arrange a meeting with one of my superiors so that her outfit could be reimbursed by my people.

After a day or two I took my platoon leader, Karol Niewiarowski, Starter, to meet with Dzidka, whom I called, according to Polish custom, my aunt. They met at Janina's place. I was told to wait outside. After a few minutes, Starter told me that he had paid the debt to Dzidka, and, looking closely at me, he added, "Why didn't you tell us that you are Jewish?" I did not answer because one did not talk about such matters, but I realized that Starter, a son of a typical country squire (*szlachcic*), had easily recognized Dzidka's distinctly Jewish features. Thank God, not everybody had his well-developed ethnic sensibilities. Afterward, I thought about this incident a lot. I am sure that it eventually led to my decision to write *Christians in the Warsaw Ghetto*.

I returned to my studies to prepare for high school final exams. On June 6, we learned about the Allied landing in Normandy. By then I was sick in bed with a bad case of scabies (Polish *świerzb*, German *Krätze*), a typical prison affliction caused by a kind of lice, called itch mites, that burrow under the skin, depositing their eggs. The hatching eggs caused terrible itching and a fever. The cure consisted of being smeared with an ill-smelling grease and waiting a few days.

I passed those few days in my small room, dreaming about the Allied forces that would soon arrive in Warsaw. While waiting for them, I studied Latin grammar like mad. I passed my high school exams at the end of June. Because of the *konspiracja* the exams consisted only of oral tests. I remember that I again made anti-German-language remarks, in German, during my German exam. I also remember that an old chemistry teacher was present at all the exams. That was important because after the war I received an official high school diploma based on his affidavit stating that I had passed my exams.

THE UPRISING

I don't remember much about the days before the Uprising. In Warsaw we expected military action any minute. As second in command of our squad, I knew that there was a house in Mokotów designated as a meeting place, with our weapons hidden nearby. What I do remember about the end of July 1944 was the rapid advance of the Red Army, the news accounts of the attempt on Hitler's life, and the increasingly chaotic behavior of the German troops. In the last days of July, we saw them running west over bridges on the Vistula. To me, they looked much like the Polish army in September 1939.

Our group kept in close contact at that time. I remember that I was very worried that we would not get to fight. A report spread through our information lines that we were going to leave the city and go into the forest. A few days before August 1, I met a good family friend, Andrzej Bogucki (an actor, who with his wife, Janina Godlewska, had saved Władysław Szpilman, whose experiences are depicted in the film *The Pianist*). He asked me what was going on (he certainly suspected that I was involved with the *konspiracja*), and I told him that "we" were probably going to leave the city. Because of this bit of information he decided to stay in Warsaw.

At the very end of July the German authorities issued an announcement demanding that all men between the ages of sixteen and sixty appear with spades to help in the construction of defensive installations. Nobody showed up, but the announcement heightened tensions in the city and, in effect, made all adult men "illegal." It is strange to me that in the hundreds of documents about the history of the Uprising this fact is seldom mentioned.

Bronek came to see me in Warsaw. He told me that he wanted to join the resistance. I became the wise older brother and told him that Franek and I would suffice. If Franek and I were killed, he should remain in the country and maintain the Dembowski family line. Since Bronek became a priest, it is lucky that Franek and I survived .

If I remember correctly, on Friday, July 28, we had the first general alarm, but it was called off. At about two o'clock in the afternoon on Tuesday, August 1, came the second and last call for mobilization. I got the message through a carefully preestablished line of communication: "Go immediately to such-and-such address in Mokotów." I was not very far from Słoeczna Street, but I took a streetcar going south on Puławska Street. We were told to wear a jacket and cap, although it was a hot day. Caps were a military requirement: in the Polish tradition, one cannot salute without wearing a cap. On the streetcar I saw several young fellows dressed like me. We smiled knowingly at each other. The mobilization of the underground army—the gathering at assembly points close to the hidden arms—was tantamount to the un-conspiracy of the conspiracy. I went near my assembly point, a small apartment building close to a school occupied by the SS (it might have been on Woronicz Street).

Grom soon arrived with the weapons, which must have been hidden in the basement of the building. Half of us had firearms: machine pistols, hand guns, or rifles. The other half, whom we called "grenadiers," had various kinds of hand grenades or self-igniting gasoline bottles (Molotov cocktails). Since I was second in command of the squad, I received a German submachine gun, a Schmeisser. I was very proud of it.

What I remember from the first seconds of fighting, which began at exactly five o'clock, was that I was terribly hot and that Grom gave me a rucksack with some food and ammunition and two heavy British antitank bombs made of plastic explosive called Gammons. With my heavy rucksack I could hardly move. We were told (even before the Uprising) that our objective would probably be the school building. Some of us came out of the house; some tried to get to the windows in the apartments giving on to the school. The poor owners went to hide in the basement, leaving their doors locked. Grom or I cleared the stairs and threw a grenade at the landing: all the doors opened immediately. We were learning our army trade very fast.

I burst into an apartment right after Grom. He fired a shot or two but immediately received a shot in the chest under his right arm. He had to leave us and go to the first-aid post. I was absolutely petrified, not by his wound, but by the realization that I was now squad leader. We exchanged fire with the SS men in the school. They fired like mad; we tried to be careful not to waste our ammunition. If I remember correctly, at about seven o'clock the Germans began to sneak out of the building in small groups under heavy protective machine-gun fire. That was our victory.

I remember very little of what happened during the next forty-eight hours. Most of the details are lost in a nightmarish fog. I got the order to follow my platoon, the third platoon, led by Lieutenant Starter. Somehow my squad got separated from him. We learned later that on the first night, Starter, along with some of our people, was killed in the attack on the Okęcie airfield, which was well defended by the German Luftwaffe.

I spent part of that first night in the square, which was then named, symbolically, Plac Trylogii (Trilogy Square), after Sienkiewicz's patriotic novel, with streets off the square, like the spokes of a wheel, named after the fictional heroes . Later that night or maybe the next day, I met up with Cygan and the rest of the third platoon. With my squad, we numbered more than thirty men. We started to move south into the Czerniaków district. We spent the second night in a small barn belonging to a peasant worker. I was glad to have people of higher rank with me; besides Cygan, Gard was there. I remember vaguely that in the evening there was a question of a local suspicious character who may have been spying on us in this no-man's-land.

In the morning there was heavy rain, and we were attacked from the south by Germans and a good number of Russian auxiliaries. I had a perfect opportunity (the only perfect opportunity in the whole of my Uprising experience) to fire on several soldiers, but my Schmeisser jammed. I have had many nightmares about this since then. My Schmeisser could fire a single shot but not a series. Because I was a squad leader I was able to quickly exchange this unreliable gun for an absolutely sure-shot rifle (a German Mauser identical to the Mauser of the Polish army). I carried this faithful rifle to the bitter end, burying it in the sewers just before coming up to surrender.

During the rain on the third day we withdrew closer to Mokotów. The situation was, to say the least, fluid. In the afternoon one of our patrols captured a truck driven by an Austrian officer. I did not take part in the capture of the truck (which, as often happens in war, took a wrong turn and drove right into our territory), but as a "Pawiak boy" with a knowledge of German, I was entrusted with guarding the prisoner. I took my cap off to show him my hair, which was still very short, and told him that I had spent some time in the SS prison. He responded by saying something like, "Gestapo sind für mich keine Geschwister!" (Gestapo people are not my brothers!). He spent the rest of the afternoon in my company. He was scared and very polite to me, and he showed no inclination to flee. I write about "my" lieutenant in part to correct the account of this incident by Lesław Bartelski in *Mokotów 1944* (Warsaw, 1972). Bartelski bestows on me the honor of capturing the truck.

During the evening of that day, we went back close to the initial place of our action, in the northeastern part of Mokotów. Our company was apparently all in one place. Cygan officially became our platoon leader when we learned that Starter was dead. Later in the action, Cygan went to another platoon, and Gard replaced him. For a squad leader like me, the platoon leader was the only important military contact. I knew the company commander, "Jacek," but he was a higher-up who did not play any real role in our lives.

On our platoon's return to Mokotów, I learned that we were cut off from the city center and the main AK force. We did not realize at first that from then on we would be engaged chiefly in a defensive action. My squad was placed at the extreme northeastern part of our territory. I remember that for several days my squad was positioned in a building at the corner of Puławska and Grażyna Streets. The construction of the building, begun in 1939, had been interrupted by the war—it had no windows, doors, or roof—and we were there for several days. We watched the Germans' movements like hawks; they did not attack our position directly, although they fired at us from time to time.

I remember seeing bodies of German soldiers and Polish civilians lying in Puławska Street, between the Germans and us. The weather was hot, and the odor was terrible. Some kind of understanding between our command and the Germans must have been reached because one morning a group of German Red Cross women removed the German bodies and covered the others with lime.

My squad was composed basically of those who had joined us in *konspiracja*. If I remember correctly, some of my boys missed the mobilization assembly point, and some were wounded on our Czerniaków "expedition." One died on the day of our arrival back in Mokotów; he shot himself accidentally while we were cleaning our weapons. From that moment on, we were extremely careful when handling guns. Our squad grew to about sixteen men when we were joined by other fighters who had gotten separated from their units during the mobilization.

For a while there were two older men in my squad. One of the men was Zbigniew Florczak; the other man, whose name I have forgotten, was his friend. They had a "prewar," right-wing outlook on the world. Florczak wrote about himself early in the Communist period in his autobiography, *Autoportret z rubinem* (Self-Portrait with a Ruby) (Warsaw, 1960), in which he talked about our squad. Generally speaking, he considered us an inferior bunch in comparison with himself. We were naive in his eyes. He also described the subsergeant Syn as "very ugly"; I suppose he knew what he was talking about since he was trained as an art historian.

Florczak and his friend apparently came to us from a nationalist group in *konspiracja* that became part of the NSZ (Narodowe Siły Zbrojne, National Armed Forces), but I know that some Communist troops from the AL (People's Army) were with us. I got to know the two men in the Stalag. Both were far more politically sophisticated than the rest of us. After the war they returned voluntarily to Poland and made reasonable careers for themselves in the Communist establishment.

As I said, the Germans did not attack our position in Mokotów, though they attacked the town from the east and the south. Our main action was to watch their nearby positions and patrol the no-man's-land at night in order to find out what they were up to. By now, we were quite good at patrolling and other basic infantry skills. The long, largely theoretical training certainly paid off after a few days of action. I remember well one such patrol, which was led by Piotruś, commander of the second platoon. There were at least six of us. We were well armed, and our boots were wrapped in rags to muffle the sound of our footsteps. We called those rags *cichołazy* (soft-walkers) and found them quite practical.

During this patrol, we went deep into no-man's-land and laid down, some distance apart, in a garden very near the German lines, close to a street going west to east. After a few minutes of absolute silence, we heard several Germans walking east on that street. They were talking among themselves, not suspecting our presence. Being well trained, we waited for Piotruś's command, but nothing happened. The Germans passed in front of us without incident. We liked Piotruś, so we did not insist on an explanation for his failure to give a command. I thought later that he must have dropped off to sleep for a few seconds. This was the closest that I got to the enemy without firing a shot and without being fired upon.

Sometime later, we were told that the Germans in the position right in front of us were fortifying the ZOM complex (Zakład Oczyszczania Miasta, City Cleaning Works) as their forward post. The complex consisted of a big brick building and a large, chiefly wooden garage and shop that faced our position. I received an order from Gard to set fire to the complex. I was in charge, and with me were my pre-Uprising friend Jan Nycz ("Lubicz") and two other fighters, "Bela" and his sidekick "Młot." (I met Lubicz again in San Francisco in the 1960s. He had become an architect in the United States.) We took a couple of big cans of gasoline and two self-igniting bottles. Very slowly and carefully, we approached the south wall of the shop and poured the gasoline on the shop's wooden wall. Bela and Młot withdrew. Lubicz and I threw the bottles and pulled back. The explosion brought an immediate reaction from the Germans: they started firing mortars. Several explosions went off close to us, forcing us to drop to the ground and crawl toward our position. Suddenly a mortar fell between Lubicz and me, but fortunately it was a dud. Lubicz said loudly, "Watch out, they're throwing bricks at us." Later we found this remark extremely funny. But if the mortar had not been a dud, neither Lubicz nor I would have survived.

All four of us came back to our lines and found our guys shooting at those Germans who were trying unsuccessfully to extinguish the fire. The wind blew the flames into the main ZOM building. That night I was very happy, admiring "my" fire. Gard came to our quarters and congratulated me, outlining a small cross on my chest with his finger and saying that I would receive "a cross." I learned after the war, when the Communist regime became less unfriendly toward the AK, that I was awarded the Cross of Valor twice (the first one for Pawiak). At the beginning of September, I think, I was promoted to the rank of subsergeant (*plutonowy*).

Sometime during September a large number of Allied planes dropped parachutes over Warsaw. I remember at least two such drops, one British and one American. We thought at first that these were troops but quite soon realized the planes were dropping supplies. Our joy at seeing the Allied planes is difficult to express. "They remember us! They remember us!," we shouted. Apparently some of the containers reached the Germans, for later, in the first hour of my captivity, I saw the German gendarmes carrying Sten guns. My squad also received a Sten gun from the first drop.

As we found out years later, the airdrops turned out to be important for other reasons. The German command in Warsaw must have been impressed by this concrete (and costly) demonstration of solidarity by the Western Allies. (The flights were perilous because the Soviets had refused to give permission for the Allied planes to land on Soviet-occupied territory.) Since the beginning of the Allied campaign in France, Gen. Dwight D. Eisenhower had been broadcasting appeals to the Germans, by radio and by dropping leaflets, to treat the soldiers of the underground armies, recognized by legal governments in exile, as regular combatants. The appeals clearly stated that those Germans who did not do so would be treated as war criminals. The concept of war criminal (*Kiegsverbrecher*) was spelled out at this time. This must have weighed heavily on the minds of the German commanders in Warsaw when they decided to enter into negotiations with the AK about capitulation. The Allied raids probably saved the lives of captured AK soldiers.

It was around this time that Kasia, our platoon's messenger, and I became well acquainted. I already knew Kasia from the Bursa, and I had met her several times in *konspiracja* activities. Everybody liked her. She was very pretty, lively, witty, and intelligent. Before the war, her father had run a private boarding school in the part of Poland that the Germans incorporated directly into the Reich. Fortunately for him, he became a prisoner of war. I say "fortunately," because the Germans killed many Polish schoolteachers in the western territory. Kasia did her job as *łączniczka* very well. She saw to it that we received antidysentery remedies (usually grated apples with red wine), that our underwear was washed, and that our gray overalls, which became our regular uniforms in mid-August, were more or less well fitted. In short, she took care of many details of daily life. And of course she carried out her main function, taking messages to different parts of our company. Everybody, including me, loved her.

Let me generalize a bit about the emotional life of us soldiers. Generally, we were divided into two age groups: the very young, ages seventeen to twenty, who because of the war missed the usual teenage experiences of ordinary life; and those who were in their early twenties or older in 1944, so had lived their teenage years before the war. The first, larger group consisted of boys, including me, who mostly just dreamed about women and often felt a sort of puppy love for any woman, especially one who was older. The second group, on the other hand, had a richer emotional life, spurred on by the constant danger and tension of the war. There were many ardent but discreet affairs among this older group, and even some marriages.

Sometime in September I learned that Kasia had been wounded by a sniper. By then, both sides in Warsaw had many sharpshooters. Her wound was, as we called it then, "idiotic." One afternoon she was sitting on a balcony with our mutual friend Janusz Bielski (Marek), unaware that the balcony could be seen by a German sniper. She was shot in the thigh by a type of bullet that fragments inside the body. Kasia's wound was not life-threatening, but it was slow-healing and painful. Many years after the war she had to have tiny bits of the shattered bullet surgically removed.

Kasia had a preliminary operation at St. Elisabeth Sisters Hospital (Szpital Elżbietanek) but was moved closer to us, thus closer to the front lines, because German artillery and the Luftwaffe constantly attacked the hospital, one of the biggest buildings in the center of Mokotów. Kasia shared a basement room with another wounded girl. Considering the horrible conditions of September 1944, she was more or less comfortable and was well cared for by friends. Since the Germans did not use heavy artillery (or planes) close to their own lines, we on the front line were in a paradoxical situation: we were safer than the people in the rear.

I visited Kasia as often as I could in the next few days. We shared a few quiet hours of bittersweet emotions, and we confessed that that we had been interested in each other even in the good old days of the Bursa. I made vague and romantic plans to become a forest ranger, an understandable yearning for someone in the noise, stench, and dirt of wartime Mokotów. I am sure that Kasia was more of an adult emotionally than I was.

On our squad's last night in Mokotów, when we were already lined up to enter the sewers, I received a few minutes' leave and went to her basement room. Before entering, I suddenly lost my courage. I heard her talking about trivial matters, and I realized that she did not know about our serious situation. I could not tell her that we were soon going into the sewers and leaving our wounded to the mercy of the German army. I left without saying good-bye.

This is the only secret that I kept from Kasia after the war. We met several times in Paris and in Poland. She became an acoustic engineer and worked for some time in France. I saw her again on the fiftieth anniversary of the Uprising. Now in our seventies, we talked at length about our puppy love days. I, for one, talked about our sweet-sad experience without regret. Kasia died suddenly of heart failure not long after.

Back to 1944. One night we learned that Piotruś had been seriously wounded in an attack on the German positions in Skarpa, a park in eastern Mokotów. Leading his platoon's attack, he received several bullets in his right arm, which had to be amputated immediately. I went to see him as soon as I could. He was in a primitive, improvised hospital. I arrived right after his operation. He was fully conscious and probably still full of adrenaline, because as soon as he saw me he said in his famous, and only slightly diminished, loud voice, "From now on, you must give me your *left* hand to shake." I believe this was the last time that I saw him in Mokotów.

My teacher and friend Marian Wichrzycki (Sword) was killed on one of the last days in Mokotów. I never saw him during the Uprising and learned about his death when I was in captivity.

I was extremely lucky during my service in Mokotów. Unlike many of my comrades from Baszta and from other units that got to Mokotów right after the start of the Uprising, until the last week of fighting my squad was not involved in heavy action, and when it was involved it was chiefly as support. But I remember that the second platoon of that company, led by my friend Grom, had a very hard fight on its hands. My brother Franek (Dzwonek) led one of the squads of that platoon.

During the the last days in Mokotów, we sustained a German attack on our position from the west and south. We defended ourselves quite well. There was heavy machine-gun fire, and we responded carefully but sparingly on account of our short supply of ammunition. At about five o'clock in the afternoon, I was ordered to take the advance line. After a few minutes of a relatively little fire, my luck still held: the Germans began to withdraw. I believe that the careful use of our weapons and good defense in general convinced the Germans that we were more numerous and better armed than we really were.

In and Out of the Sewers

One late afternoon—I think it was September 28—we were told that in the evening we would attempt to evacuate to the city center (Śródmieście) via the sewers. Our company, I believe, was one of the last to go into the sewers. We knew, of course, that messengers and even small units of soldiers had been using the sewers between Mokotów and the city center.

I remember our unsuccessful passage through the sewers as a nightmare. Immediately we found ourselves in a narrow pipe, which was very difficult to get through. We were told to leave behind everything except our weapons. I had on only my overalls, my shoes, and my German helmet. I dragged my faithful Mauser with me. To protect my watch from the water in the sewer, I moved it above my elbow. (This did not protect my watch from the water, but it did protect it from the Germans after the surrender.) After getting through the narrow pipe, we arrived at the larger storm sewer. We were in darkness, walking bent over, stopping and starting. Again and again, we passed the word from the front to the rear and from the rear to the front. Occasionally somebody who was in the back was allowed to move ahead. Very soon, I realized that the level of the sewer water was steadily rising. Even then I understood that the Germans had blown up or blocked the sewer in front of us. I remember several times I walked over drowned bodies lying in the water.

I began to be less and less aware of my surroundings. I felt absolutely alone. I had regular visions of light. One of the most memorable hallucinations was the sight of a large, sumptuous, and well-lit hall. I got up, hitting my helmet on the vault of the sewer. I filled my helmet with sewer water and poured it on my head; the hallucinations ceased for a while. Later, a doctor told us that many soldiers had these hallucinations and that they were caused by the rising level of the water and consequently diminishing amount of oxygen, and harmful gases. Even now, after seventy years, I cross to the other side of the street when I see an open manhole.

Suddenly I heard the order, "Dzwonek to the front!" (Dzwonek do przodu!). "Dzwonek" was Franek's pseudonym. He was a squad leader in the second platoon (I was in the third platoon). After a while he passed me and went forward. He had no idea why he had been called up front. For some reason, someone thought he had special knowledge of the sewers ahead. Later he crawled back and joined me. We were exhausted. It was our second night without sleep and our second day without food. I passed in and out of consciousness.

All at once I saw the manhole above us open. I heard the harsh German cry, "Alle raus!" (Everybody out!), and saw a hand holding a grenade. I put my rifle in a small connecting pipe and climbed up and out of the manhole. I realized that it was afternoon; we must have spent at least eighteen hours in the sewers. We were surrounded not by regular soldiers but by gendarmes (*Schutzpolizei*). We were close to their barracks on Dworkowa Street. My first reaction was elation at the light and clean air. We were told to lie down on the ground.

Nearby, the gendarmes were shooting some of our comrades, those who had come out of the sewers before us. I recognized a member of my squad, Drozd (his family name was Judejko). I still have this image before my eyes: Drozd was standing, and when a single shot was fired he leaped in the air and crumpled on the ground. We expected to be shot too, but I was too tired to feel fear. That is a real blessing that comes from absolute physical exhaustion. Franek was perhaps less exhausted and certainly stronger than I, because he said quietly to the fellows around him, "We should shout something, like, 'Long live Poland!'" I agreed, and I think that all the other fellows agreed with him too, but I was too tired to answer.

After a long wait, the German gendarmes were replaced by Wehrmacht soldiers. We were told to get in formation three deep, and we began a long march. Our destination, it turned out, was the temporary camp in Pruszków, some ten miles west of Warsaw. The group in which I found myself had about two hundred men. Dzwonek again encouraged everyone to march like soldiers: "Heads up, and keep in step." On the march to Pruszków, our column was passed by at least two military trucks carrying former German prisoners from Mokotów. They wore civilian clothes with a large *N* (for *Niemiec*, "German") painted on their chests and their backs. We had needed their uniforms. When they saw us, some of them made threatening gestures with their fists.

On arrival in Pruszków we were put in an abandoned factory. I do not remember whether we received any food. Again, our total exhaustion made us indifferent to anything but sleep. The first night, I slept on the cement, without any covering. I was wearing only my stinking, but by then almost dry, overalls.

After I had slept, my *konspiracja* instincts came into play with full force. We had no idea of our fate, but we expected the worst. Therefore, I tore to bits my AK identification card, given to me at the beginning of the Uprising, my "miraculous" pass from the Gestapo, and all the other papers I had in my possession. I deposited them carefully into the outdoor latrine.

Only after the capitulation of the city center on October 2 did we learn about our High Command's negotiations with General von dem Bach Zelewski about surrender. We also learned that the negotiations included the soldiers in Mokotów. We were thus granted combatant status, which meant that we were protected by the Geneva Convention concerning prisoners of war.

This became certain when we were taken to the regular transit camp built for Soviet prisoners of war in Skierniewice. We arrived there in cattle wagons and met our comrades from the city center. We immediately realized how poor we Mokotów fellows were. We had nothing except our awful tattered overalls. The fighters from the city center, having capitulated after a brief ceasefire, went into captivity more or less well dressed. (Only those who wore German uniforms had to give them up.) If we looked like beggars, they looked, as the German press said, like *die stoltze Polen* (proud Poles).

From the time of our march to Pruszków, we were guarded only by members of the Wehrmacht—no SS, no gendarmes. The Germans allowed local populations and the RGO to help us. Finally, I was given soup and bread in generous quantities. For the last three weeks of fighting in Mokotów we had been on what could only be described as meager rations. Many of our patrols involved finding vegetables and potatoes in the little private gardens (*działki*) in no-man's-land and bringing them back to our lines. The RGO people in Skierniewice fed us and took our names. All these civilians were kind and sympathetic to us. I shall never forget them. I threw on the ground a brief message addressed to my relatives in Brzeźce. It was copied onto a postcard and delivered there. After the war, I kept it as a souvenir.

In Skierniewice, some Gestapo officers visited our camp. But since we were in the custody of the Wehrmacht, they had no authority. They were hoping that we would hand over the Jews among us. There were in fact some Jews in our group, but we did not want to talk to the Gestapo about them. I remember one incident in which a Gestapo officer recognized a former prisoner whom he had interrogated. This young Polish officer, by then sure of the protection of the Geneva Convention, ignored the *konspiracja* rules of acting like an idiot and saying nothing and talked to the Gestapo man. I remember that he said he had joined the AK in 1940.

After a few days in Skierniewice, we were loaded into freight trains to begin the long journey to a Stalag at the other end of Germany. My Mokotów days were definitely over, and my career as a prisoner of war was beginning.

Old and New Thoughts on the Uprising

I want to say a few words about the Uprising from a purely personal point of view. Our morale during the *konspiracja* and the fighting was very high. We were convinced that our cause was just. Every act of mistreatment, every German roundup of the civilian population, every public execution, and every daily personal humiliation wrought by individual German soldiers strengthened this conviction. For me and for many others, the Nazi elimination of the Jewish population persuaded us that the Germans would stop at nothing to eliminate the Poles as well.

Our most basic desire for human dignity played into our drive to join the *konspiracja* and to fight to restore Warsaw as the capital of Poland. Thus when rumors began to fly that we were to leave the city and go to the forest, and especially when a premature mobilization on July 28 was called off, we soldiers were distressed.

Our morale, of course, had plenty to do with the Polish insurrectional ethos. We, the youth born in an independent Poland, certainly shared in that ethos. But when we lost after more than sixty days of fighting, we began to question the reasons for and wisdom of insurrection. I want to touch briefly on these questions, not as a politician or an important leader, but as a simple and perhaps typical foot soldier in the *konspiracja* and in the Uprising.

To me, the impetus for the *konspiracja*, which began in Warsaw even before the capitulation of Poland in 1939, was the armed struggle against the occupier that would culminate in a general, open struggle. The German occupation, based in large part on the racist principles of Germanic superiority over the Slavic masses, practically forced us to organize and prepare for the struggle to reclaim Poland.

The strongly insurrectional character of the AK was powerfully strengthened by the destruction of the Polish Jews, of which we were well aware. After the summer of 1942 and the heroic but hopeless Jewish uprising in the Warsaw Ghetto, the Germans became absolute enemies.

We were certain, too, that the Russians, our allies and certainly the allies of our allies, shared our desire for active resistance. It was inconceivable that they would disapprove of our armed uprising in Warsaw. My teacher Wicher was an exception; as a former Communist, he knew the real Stalin better than most of us. In 1944 insurrection was in the air. Soviet radio and the propaganda that emanated from the Communists among us convinced us that the Uprising was what they wanted. The military units of the AL, organized by the Communists, were with us in Warsaw, as was the civilian population. The presence of the AL in Warsaw renders ridiculous the postwar Communist propaganda that the Uprising was "anti-Soviet."

Soviet propaganda had always encouraged armed resistance. Every radio transmission from the Soviet Union had always begun with the phrase, "Death to the German-Fascist invaders." I heard this slogan in Polish, in Russian, and in French. I will never forget the melodious, sexy voice of the French-language Moscow radio announcer sweetly insisting, "Mort aux envahisseurs allemands!" The call to arms was heard not only in the East but in the West too. From June 1944 on, we knew that the slogan of the powerful French Communist Party and their partisans was "Pas de libération sans insurrection" (No liberation without insurrection). Paris was liberated with the active help of the French Underground in the third week of the Warsaw Uprising.

We knew, of course, that there could be political problems with the relationship between the London government and the newly organized Polish Committee of National Liberation, but it was unthinkable that the armed struggle of the AK would not be not supported by the Red Army. When the Polish troops from the Soviet side crossed the Vistula without too much difficulty, when I saw a Soviet artillery officer (dressed like a Polish streetcar conductor) directing the artillery fire beyond Warsaw, when we heard the (false) rumors that the Russians were close by on Litewska Street, my companions and I believed that sooner or later the Soviet army would come to help us against the common enemy. It was a former American Communist, Edmund Wilson, who, sometime in the late 1940s, summed up the Soviet stand in Warsaw as Stalin's first step in the Cold War.

In 1967 my brother Bronek took me to visit his boss and friend, Cardinal Stefan Wyszyński. During a conversation with the cardinal in Warsaw, he asked, "Why did you rise in Warsaw?" I answered by posing another question: "What would the Communists have done if we had not risen?" And then I tried to answer this question myself: "They would certainly have started a general police suppression of the AK on the grounds that since we did not want to fight the Germans, we were not anti-Nazi and must have been anti-Soviet. After all, in 1946, in Moscow, the last commandant of the AK was condemned for collaborating with the Nazis." The cardinal listened in silence, and we did not discuss the matter further. But later I found this idea presented in one of his writings.

It was only at the end of September 1944 that my close friends and I began to realize that Stalin had decided to punish the Polish insurgents by staying on the east side of Vistula. But even then we could not really accept our doubts about the Soviets' intentions.

I believe that the Russian stand on the Vistula was a mistake from the point of view of the Soviet state and its long-range interests. It is true that the death of Warsaw and the death or captivity of thousands of bright, young Polish resisters made the immediate formation of the Communist government easier. Polish losses are calculated now as 150,000 civilians killed, 18,000 fighters killed, and about 20,000 taken prisoner. The efficacy of the forty years of Polish Communist rule was profoundly handicapped by the Soviets' behavior in Poland between 1939 and 1944. The mass arrests and deportations in the early 1940s of the populations from the eastern part of prewar Poland to the depths of the Soviet Union, the mass murder in Katyń of Polish officers, and, above all, the passivity of the Soviet army at the gates of Warsaw were insurmountable obstacles to more or less "normal" coexistence and cooperation between the broadly based Polish population and its Soviet neighbor.

Collaboration with the insurgents against the common foe would have diminished the sense of injury over other 1939–44 Soviet actions and would have created a climate of Polish opinion in which there would have been a real chance to construct a far more genuine political relationship. After all, the Soviets had such a relationship with the Czechoslovak government (at least until 1948). We realized later that Stalin had created what he wanted: a vassal relationship between him and the puppet governments. This relationship fell apart in 1989, after forty-five years of lies. It doubtless precipitated the fall of the Soviet Union itself. On August 1, 2014, Poland celebrated the seventieth anniversary of the Warsaw Uprising. I was invited to participate. I found that the collapse of the Communist regime in 1989 was universally explained as a result of the 1944 Uprising. All the signs celebrating the anniversary bore not two but three dates: 1944–1989–2014.

STALAG XB, SANDBOSTEL

The railroad trip to the prison camp was very long, with frequent stops on sidings and the sound of Allied bombers. We passed through a damaged country smelling of defeat. Everywhere we stopped, most of the people we encountered were foreign slave workers. They encouraged us. I remember a fellow in a German railroad uniform who told us in pure Silesian Polish, "Don't you worry, he [Hitler] has had it."

We were very thirsty and hungry during the journey. In Berlin we got some soup from women of the German Red Cross. One such *Schwester* was young and pretty, and her face, her blue eyes, expressed such compassion that, even then, I could not embrace anti-German feelings.

Late one afternoon, we arrived at a station called Bremerförde. It was west of Bremen in the northwestern tip of Germany. We walked several kilometers to the camp, Stalag XB, near the village of Sandbostel. It was a huge camp, in the middle of the northern moorlands (*Heide*). It held thousands of French, Belgian, British, and Yugoslav NCOs and, in a separate and unequal compound, Soviet prisoners.

The Soviets were extremely poor. They did not receive any support from outside, were mistreated by their own *Lagerpolizei,* and had to do the worst jobs in the camp. I soon realized that the Soviet soldiers were not being treated as prisoners of war because the Soviet Union had not signed the Geneva Convention governing the fate of POWs. The clothing of the Soviet prisoners was marked, not with the letters KGF (for *Kriegsgefangener,* "prisoner of war") like ours, but with SU (Soviet Union). They were constantly tempted with the promise of food to join the Russian Liberation Army of General Andrey Vlasov, which was fighting on the Nazi side. I saw at least one group of Soviet prisoners leaving the camp for Vlasov's army in the late fall of 1944.

It is difficult to understand the power of hunger, the hunger that forced those poor men to choose the obviously losing side. But they also joined Vlasov out of desperation: Stalin took a dim view of Soviet soldiers who had "allowed" themselves to be taken prisoner. One must understand Stalin's ruthless treatment of his own people who were taken by force to Germany during the war to understand his attitude to the Warsaw Uprising.

There were also several hundred Polish prisoners who had been held since 1939, all of them NCOs, who looked at our dirty rags and our belligerent attitudes with horror. One of them told me later, "You looked as if you were ready to fight again." I thought that it was a compliment, but it was not. This man had been beaten down by five years of captivity, and he thought that we were foolish. They constantly asked the accusatory question, "Why did you rise in Warsaw?" As far as we knew, there were never any plans to put the Polish prisoners of 1944 together with those of 1939. The latter were well settled in the Stalag with their few possessions, their LPs (a gift of the YMCA), and their quiet, monotonous life of waiting.

As soon as we arrived in Stalag XB, we were registered, photographed, and issued dog tags. Mine read: XB221857. I remember that a civilian German photographer took our picture with a simple Leica camera. Several prisoners in three rows were taken in one shot. We kept our prison numbers written on a small blackboard on our chests. Very soon after settling into Sandbostel, most of the prisoners of lower rank were taken to distant work groups (*Arbeitskommando*), and some officers, like Jacek, commander of Company B1, who were initially with us were sent to the officers' camp.

We Mokotów guys acquired some clothes from our fellow prisoners, but we were still pretty ragged. After a few weeks, the Germans communicated to us through the leader of the 1939 Polish prisoners, who bore the title *Vertrauensmann* (Spokesman), that we would receive old German uniforms. There was a large tailor shop in our camp where chiefly Polish prisoners cleaned and patched German uniforms apparently arriving from military hospitals.

We were happy about getting clothing, because our overalls were not adequate against the damp and cold northwestern German moorland. Each of us was supposed to bring all of his clothes and exchange them for the German stuff. But we were terribly camp-wise already, and we went to the collection point half-naked. The German staff sergeant ordered us to wait. After three hours in freezing weather, we received our German clothing. I got German army pants, a jacket, and an overcoat. The jacket was repaired; it looked as if its former owner had been shot in the chest.

Our uniform adventures continued. At the beginning of 1945, the Red Cross sent brand-new American uniforms, but all of them, including the greatcoats, were of World War I vintage. Right after liberation a small group of us hitchhiked to Italy. On seeing us, an American soldier exclaimed, "Oh my God, you must have been in the prison camp a long time!" He told us that we looked like Sergeant York, the legendary World War I infantryman. But in the camp our clean uniforms and soldierlike appearance were good for morale.

We were very hungry and very poor, but our dignity depended on cleanliness and smartness of bearing. We soon realized that if an individual was not taking care of his appearance and ceased to wash, it meant that he was weakening physically and in serious danger of becoming mortally ill. The 1939 Polish prisoners were good examples of smart military bearing, and in that they certainly were models for us.

But in our camp the militarily smartest, both in dress and in behavior, were the British. The British addressed one another as "Kriegie," slang for *Kriegsgefangener*. Most of them, I learned later, were guardsmen taken at Dunkirk. For the most part, the German *Wachmänner* (guards) were World War I veterans, in their sixties; the few younger men had been wounded or suffered from frostbite in Russia. They showed great respect for the British. The British usually acted as if Germans were not there.

We Warsaw fellows were placed initially in uncomfortable quarantine barracks, separated from the camp by a wire fence. The British came to the fence to speak to us in a primitive camp, or pidgin, German (*Lagerdeutsch*). I remember one phrase, "Dein Haus?" (Your house?), which meant "Where are you from?," "What is your nationality?"

When encountering a German officer, prisoners were required to salute. The British complied but in such a sloppy way that some of the German officers became angry, especially when they saw them salute each other and us with a real guardsman's smartness. In addition, when addressed by a German officer, the British prisoners feigned ignorance of German, whereupon the officer shouted, "Dolmetscher!" (Interpreter!). Immediately the British prisoners would begin to chant, "Dolmetscher, Dolmetscher, Dolmetscher," until an intellectual-looking fellow with thick glasses appeared unhurriedly and started to speak in a German worthy of a Heidelberg seminar.

The Germans were almost as short of cigarettes as we were. (We received some in the International Red Cross parcels.) When the British passed through the gates that separated the various parts of the camp, they would often tip the German guards with a cigarette—a subtle putdown.

The most numerous prisoners were the French. All of them were NCOs but reservists rather than professional soldiers. In the camp I had plenty of opportunities to improve my French during my frequent missions to the French compound. I liked many of the French prisoners. By the time we got to the camp, practically all of French territory was occupied by the Allies and De Gaulle was the head of the government, so the French were unable to receive food parcels from home.

I was surprised to see portraits of Marshal Pétain prominently displayed in the French barracks. Since August 1944 Pétain had been a guest-prisoner of the Germans in Sigmaringen, and my fellow Poles and I did not understand this fidelity. But then neither did we understand their attitude to the war in general.

I knew many individual French prisoners who were quite depressed, but as a group they tried to maintain a cheerful front. The German officers liked to hear the French prisoners sing when they were moving in formation. I learned one French camp song, or rather its refrain, obviously not understood by the Germans. The sense of the song was this: "The good God sitting in the high heaven noticed that his prisoners are very sad. He therefore asked his archangel Michael to compose an anthem to cheer the poor fellows up. Its refrain was sung by all: 'Dans le cul, / Dans le cul, / Ils ont la victoire. / Ils sont foutus' [In the arse, in the arse is their victory. They are fucked up]." I forget the last line of the refrain, something rhyming with *victoire*. The melody was very catchy, and the German officers obviously liked it.

The black market kings of the camp were the Belgians, all Walloons, for Hitler did not allow Germanic "brothers," that is, Flemish, Dutch, and Norwegian soldiers, to be put in prison camps. But, not surprisingly, there was a lot of black market activity among all the prisoners. Until the fall of 1944, all the prisoners (except the

Russians) received parcels from their families, in addition to those sent by the Red Cross. Janina used to send food parcels to her French cousin Landy, who, an officer, was in an *Oflag*. Apparently he was afraid to contact his own family in France because they were Jewish. Both types of parcels provided the materials of internal camp commerce. This commerce was doubtlessly abetted by the Germans, who were always trying to buy cigarettes and Nescafé from us in exchange for bread.

The commerce was quite well organized. The established "unit" of exchange in Stalag XB was one loaf of German bread (a kilogram), twenty American dollars, or one pack of American cigarettes (usually Chesterfields or Camels). I have no idea where the twenty-dollar bills came from, but I saw some of them. I remember that I sold my good watch for two "units." The watch, like its owner, had suffered in the sewers, but there was a professional watchmaker in our group of prisoners who was able to repair it so that it could be exchanged for cigarettes. I did not smoke, but the two packs of Chesterfields I received in payment for my watch kept me supplied with extra food for several days. My colleagues were happy to sell me some of their meager food for a smoke.

For us, the most important fact of camp life was hunger. We were always hungry. The only time that we had almost enough German food in the camp was the first evening. We were supposed to reach the camp in the morning, but we arrived late. Thus the food for breakfast, lunch, and dinner was given to us all at once that evening.

The daily menu never varied. Breakfast consisted of herb tea, not very hot but good for shaving; a piece of bread; a small piece of margarine; and a spoonful of marmalade, made with artificial sugar and chiefly red beets. The margarine was also ersatz; if you tried to melt it, there was so little fat that it practically evaporated. If I remember correctly, the bread ration was about one hundred grams. In order to divide the bread we used our dog tags: the width of a dog tag was about the thickness of our daily portion of bread. The bread was heavy, with many nongrain additives. The only other meal of the day consisted of a plate of soup and about three potatoes boiled in their jackets. The soup was invariably turnips boiled in salted water, with a film of grease floating on top. On Sundays the soup was better: thin oat gruel.

We learned very quickly how to divide the food fairly: the one who divides does not choose. The food arrived in buckets for twenty people. Potatoes were placed on the table in groups of three, and each group consisted of a bigger, a smaller, and a smallest potato. Twenty fellows in the room were lined up, and each had to take a portion in the order in which they were arranged on the table. Bread was also cut into equal portions, and one had to take a piece in the order in which it was displayed. Sometimes we got a portion for two people: invariably the person who divided the food in half had to offer first choice to his partner. He made very sure to divide the food evenly. Only at the beginning of our life in the Stalag did we have quarrels about dividing the food.

If a prisoner worked during the day, his ration was kept for him. Again, at the very beginning we had some cases of people stealing food and cheating when dividing the portions. A severe beating, organized by the natural leaders among us, soon discouraged these practices. We were hungry but honest. But outside the camp we tried to steal (in camp parlance, "to organize") anything even remotely edible.

It is very difficult to imagine what it is like to live on about six hundred calories a day—the generous calculation made by the medical people among us. One becomes constantly fixated on food. One cannot think about anything else. We were all about twenty years old, but the Sandbostel diet deprived us of any amorous thoughts. In our thinking and in our dreams, food replaced sex. We had very vivid food dreams. My typical dream was that I was working on the big farm in Szczyty again. In Poland the main food for fattening pigs was potatoes prepared in vast boilers and then mixed with chopped barley or oats. From time to time, I had eaten one or two of these freshly boiled potatoes. That became a motif of my food dreams: I smelled the hot potato, and I put it in my mouth, but as soon as I began to eat it, I woke up.

Let me give you a couple examples of the culture of hunger. The International YMCA had a program for prisoners of war through which the Poles received some records and books. Probably by accident, a couple of Polish books were blatantly pornographic. In those days we called them "books published in Paris." All the amorous adventures of *la princesse Fifi* and her numerous young gardeners left us absolutely cold. But we read, with enormous attention, the few pages on which Fifi ate a meal. When I read a book aloud in the camp (or, my other specialty, when I was relating the plots of films I had seen before the war), I always "stopped for a meal or two." The usual question from my attentive audience was, "And what did they have next?" Neither I nor my colleagues dreamed about complicated gourmet dishes: potatoes, pasta, and bread were the usual objects of our dreams.

Since I have spent most of my adult life as a teacher of medieval Provençal and French poetry, so much of it devoted to love and desire, let me simply say that in the camp the desire for food had completely replaced the desire for love in our literary activities. We referred to hunger as "a little longing," from the first words of the popular love song: "A little longing / But it is as vast as the whole world" (Maleńka tęsknota / A wielka jest jak cały świat). We had several song writers among us. I remember a camp composition sung to the popular prewar melody of "Tango Marina": "When we put on the darling bread / The white miracle MARGARYNA" (Gdy na chlebek się kładzie / Biały cud, MARGARYNA), with prolonged stress on the penultimate syllable, *Mariiina*.

My first cousin Paweł Matuszewski apparently suffered less from the scarcity of food than I did. It was a question not only of size—he was much smaller than I was—but probably of the nervous system in general. But I was not like the people who were completely overcome by an obsession with food; rather, I was probably somewhere in the middle on the scale of reaction to food deprivation.

But all of us suffered from the unpleasant physical side effects of too little food: constipation, a constant feeling of being cold, and a far too frequent desire to urinate: we woke several times a night to go to the latrine. We were very weak. We sat on the floor, since there was no furniture in our rooms. I remember that getting up from the floor was difficult. Usually one had to ask a friend for help. After getting up, one had to stand still for a minute because of dizziness and a feeling of heat in the head. Many of us suffered from strange illnesses. Several died from what we called "galloping tuberculosis."

Because we were NCOs we were not forced to work outside the camp, but we had to do all sorts of service jobs. The one that I remember the best was bringing supplies from the railroad station to the camp. Narrow-gauge tracks were laid down, and we pushed the supplies on small coal mine lorries, three prisoners to a lorry. If we were lucky we would get access to the food supplies. At least twice I pushed the turnips, and once (a miracle!) the bread. We could not bring anything into the camp, and I ate a whole loaf of bread without difficulty.

Work parties were invariably composed of fifteen men, carefully counted before leaving camp and on returning. The cry "Fünfzehn Mann" meant that we could come or go. Some of the prisoners used the trip to the station to escape—not permanently, of course, but to a village to exchange coffee or cigarettes for bread. Nobody thought about permanent escape. In the camp we were protected from the SS and the Gestapo, who were terrorizing the countryside, including their own population. But escaping from the fifteen-man group was easy. Our guards were old men whom we often addressed as *Vati*, "Daddy." Usually one man engaged *Vati* in a conversation while the "businessman" sneaked away. I am quite sure that at least some of the *Wachmänner* knew about the temporary escapes but knew, too, that the fellow would soon return. The war was obviously ending, and there was an inevitable relaxation of the rules and regulations.

I remember with pleasure one job on the outside. We were marching out of the camp and encountered a truck full of AK women being taken from our camp to a camp set up exclusively for female prisoners of war. When we waved at our girls, not only did they wave back, but one of them threw a pack of cigarettes to us. This time our *Wachmann* was a young fellow with badly frozen feet who wore soft felt boots and had great difficulty walking. He was very impressed by the generosity of our girls. Since everything had to be divided equally, we decided to include him in the group. Each of us received one and a quarter cigarettes. The *Wachmann* was practically moved to tears by our gift. I hope that we weakened the racial prejudices that had been ingrained in him.

After several weeks in the Stalag we received the first International Red Cross parcel. If I remember correctly, it was one parcel for two prisoners. Each parcel contained six packs of cigarettes, a small tin of Nescafé, a tin of Spam, a tin of corned beef, a tin of powdered milk, a jar of peanut butter, and some biscuits. This was the first time in my life that I tasted such incredible and hitherto unknown delectable things as peanut butter, Spam, and corned beef. I thought that peanut butter was a dessert to be eaten with a spoon.

The contents of the parcel were divided up according to the usual principle: you divide, I choose. For me it was the cigarettes and for most of the others it was the Nescafé that were strictly bartering objects. Coffee was sold to the *Wachmänner* or the German villagers for bread. Cigarettes, as I have explained, were for me simply a currency. The aid organized by the International Red Cross in Geneva was important to us. There is no doubt that receiving some substantial food from time to time was crucial to our health.

The Red Cross parcels were usually American, but once we got some from the Canadian Red Cross. They were greeted with cries of despair and gnashing of teeth, because instead of cigarettes they contained a bigger packet of biscuits. Later, when I lived in Canada, I wrote a letter to the Canadian Red Cross about it. I imagine that one of the sweet old ladies who ran the parcel program for the "boys in the camps" was an early crusader for the prohibition of tobacco. She had no idea about the cigarettes' value as the all-important camp currency.

Poles, although fully represented in the International Red Cross through their legal government in London, received fewer parcels than the U.S., British, French, and Belgian prisoners. Our 1939 comrades repeatedly pointed this out to us. For me that was a profound lesson in international politics: Central Europe is less important than the West. We used to joke, "I will make sure that the next time I become a prisoner of war, I am in the American army." I did not suspect then that I would spend my adult life as an American.

We met the American prisoners of war sometime before Christmas. They had been captured in the Battle of the Bulge at Ardennes and marched a long way to Sandbostel. They were hard hit by their sudden introduction to the German POW diet. Several were from the Detroit area and spoke some Polish. They told us they were afraid that they would die of hunger. We answered, "You'll get used to the camp, and you'll make it." Soon they received a generous number of Red Cross parcels and began to engage in the internal black market. One of the effects of the Americans' coming to our Stalag was the immediate disappearance of the $20 bills. Those clever Yanks well knew that $20 were worth a lot more than a pack of Chesterfields. The Americans stayed in Sandbostel until the end of the war. They were repatriated immediately afterward, before the French and the British.

The only other time I was not hungry in the camp was when it was my turn to work in the kitchen. The idea was that one should eat as much soup and potatoes as one could. It must have been toward the end of the war, because by then our camp had received a large number of officers evacuated from camps in eastern Germany. While handing a bucket of soup to the officers, I saw my cousin Lt. Stanisław Sierakowski, who had been taken prisoner in Warsaw. I had a short conversation with him, but we lost touch when the officers were taken someplace else.

I remember my turn in the kitchen with joy. It was a food paradise, which, I think, lasted about a week. Two Yugoslav officers saw us eating food and reported our dog tag numbers to the Germans. We were fired immediately, and a few days later I was called during the evening roll call and told that I had received an eight-day sentence in the camp lockup.

Serving a sentence in the camp prison was very hard. Although the cells, built for two, were clean and there were blankets to sleep on top of and under, we were given food only every other day. The time was thus divided into ordinary (eating) days and long (not-eating) days. I was put in the lockup twice, the second time for insulting the *Wachmann.* While he was searching our work party, I repeated the order given to the search dogs: "Such, such, such" (Seek, seek, seek).

My first time in lockup had an aspect of comedy. The spokesman for the Americans, their *Vertrauensmann,* was a German American from Ohio who was insolent and used his grandfather's German to speak to the officers, including the familiar form "du." Among other things, he also pretended not to know any polite form of address. The American prisoners of war refused to have a different *Vertrauensmann.* So this man was kept in the lockup but held regular office hours through the window. He received food from his compatriots. Since the war was winding down, the camp authorities tolerated the American's hijinks. For us, the behavior of the *amerikanischer Vertrauensmann* was a source of much satisfaction.

During my second term in lockup my cellmate was a Russian soldier my age. He had been taken prisoner in the summer of 1944 when his patrol got lost and found itself behind the German lines. He knew that Stalin never forgave his soldiers for becaming prisoners of war and was sad but resigned about the future. On one Sunday morning we heard our fellows singing religious hymns. It was Easter. We had less than a month of prison left to endure. My Russian cellmate greeted me with a traditional Orthodox greeting, "Chrystos voskres," but he added the nontraditional *"dlia tebia,"* "Christ is risen *for you.*" I assured him that Christ had risen for him too, but my poor Russian friend was not sure that I was right. He knew a lot about the Christian religion. He told me that his grandmother had taught him about it. May God keep this young man and his grandmother with him!

The Nazis were losing the war. For hours day and night we heard the roar of hundreds and hundreds of Allied bombers going into Germany. Sandbostel was located on the route from England to the center of Germany. Right after Easter, the Germans allowed us to write on the roof of our barracks in big letters: SOS POW. This was to protect us from daytime strafing by the British planes. Our camp was indeed struck but at night. One of our men was killed, and I was hit by a bomb fragment, but the blow was completely absorbed by the heavy sleeve of my World War I American greatcoat.

The last days in Stalag XB were full of excitement. The SS brought several thousand concentration camp prisoners (*Häftlinge*) from Neuengamme, one of its large *Arbeitskommandos*, to our camp and dumped them there. Himmler had ordered the SS to kill off the surviving prisoners in the concentration camps, but by this time his orders were rarely followed. This was my first direct contact with the horrors of the concentration camps. The prisoners were in an awful state and were dying in large numbers. The German officers of our Stalag asked the prisoners of war to help with the care of the new prisoners. We segregated them according to nationality, and a group of POWs was selected to take care of them. Several other Poles and I were asked to care for the Dutch since there were no Dutch POWs in our camp.

Our main task was to make sure that our meager rations reached each of the prisoners. They were beyond any state of social organization; they were fighting, with their characteristic slow-motion movement, for every scrap of food. We imposed order. Many of the prisoners did not understand who we were. In our splendid American uniforms, perhaps to them we looked like another kind of Germans. Poor as we were, we gathered some potatoes and bits of cigarettes to offer to the *Häftlinge*, a true act of charity considering the shortage of food.

I shall never forget one particular scene that I witnessed. A prisoner of war gave a *Häftling* a choice between a small potato and a quarter of a cigarette. Slowly, the prisoner chose the cigarette. He sat down on the ground, put the cigarette in his mouth, received a light from his benefactor, inhaled deeply, shook a little, and died. We, the KGF chaps, were horrified. But another *Häftling*, seeing the cigarette held tightly between the fingers of the dead man, approached slowly, removed the cigarette, and smoked it with obvious satisfaction.

In the second half of April, when our Stalag was being used increasingly as a dumping ground for all sorts of prisoners held by the Germans, we received the order to evacuate on foot to a nearby camp for the marine and merchant marine prisoners (*Marlag*) at Westertimke, which was even closer to the Dutch frontier than Sandbostel. If I remember correctly, only the Poles and the French were evacuated. Carrying our meager possessions on our backs, we marched for about eighteen hours, using the back roads. We got new *Wachmänner*, who were very polite. They addressed us as "Herren Kriegsgefangenen." The old slurs were no longer heard.

All the AK fellows kept together. We did not lose our cunning or our improvisational abilities. There was an AK chap from the Neuengamme concentration camp who had been arrested by the Germans, before the Uprising, I think. We gave him an extra American uniform and simply took him with us. The poor fellow was very happy about this improvement in his status, but he soon became faint. He had to be helped and carried a good part of the way to Westertimke.

We spent only a few days in Westertimke, and I do not remember much about this new camp. We later learned that under the Allies Sandbostel acquired the reputation, because of the late influx of the *Häftlinge*, of being a large Nazi concentration camp. Later, it became a transit camp for German POWs. It was there that Heinrich Himmler, in disguise as a simple Wehrmacht soldier, committed suicide.

FOUR

Liberation and Emigration

In Westertimke there were only a small number of Germans, and we were told to organize our own self-policing groups. We wore white armbands and carried big sticks—symbols of office. In fact, we kept pretty good military discipline while waiting to be liberated. Our camp was not situated directly on the front line, and there was not much fighting nearby. Heavy bombers were no longer flying at night, but there was a lot of strafing by the Allied planes in the daytime. Hardly any vehicle could move on the nearby highway without being attacked by light planes. Many German civilians moved close to the camp to take advantage of the protection offered by the POW SOS signs painted on the roofs of our barracks. Day and night we waited for the British to arrive.

The moment of liberation came as an anticlimax. One night, right after April 20—Hitler's birthday and thus an official holiday—I was on duty as one of the Polish "armband" people. We were waiting for the Allied army. Our *Wachmänner* were lined up at the main gate to the camp. We were right behind them, also lined up. Suddenly we heard something. Three British soldiers, who we later learned were from the Welsh Guards, came up to us. The *Wachmänner* stood at attention, but nothing happened. The leader of the British patrol explained to one of us who understood English that they could not liberate us until the next day, about noon. In the meantime, the Germans would have to be in charge, to protect us from the marauding SS troops that were nearby. I had to hand back the Mauser that one of the German guards had given to me. I became a prisoner again, and we waited.

In the end, the liberation of the camp was staged for the benefit of the film unit accompanying the Welsh Guards. At noon, the same *Wachmänner*, with the same Mausers and with the same unmilitary-looking personal gear, were lined up at the gate. Many of the prisoners were gathered behind them. First a jeep carrying the film unit arrived, then a tank rolled up and broke the main gate. We all shouted, "Hurrah! Hurrah!," and some soldiers removed the guns from the hands of the grateful Germans, who were later taken away carrying their little suitcases. A couple of British officers started to talk to our *Vertrauensmann*. We were told to maintain military discipline and to obey the British liaison officers, who would be appointed shortly. Above all, we were told not leave the camp as long as the military actions continued.

There was universal awareness of the danger of the *Wehrwolf*, that is, the German underground armed resistance. We from the AK certainly believed that *Wehrwolf* agents were in the area, but, as we would learn later, they were not. Unlike the Poles, the Germans did not have a tradition of insurrection.

For a few days, life in Westertimke continued normally, except that we had more to eat. There was quite a bit of British (white!) bread. By law, we were considered members of the Polish army, temporary prisoners of war. After about May 1, a week before the war officially ended, some of our number got in touch with the First Polish Armored Division, whose headquarters were in the nearby Dutch town of Harlem (baptized by us as Maczkowo, in honor of General Maczek, the division commander). We learned that the Second Polish Corps in Italy wanted former POWs to supplement their thinned-out ranks. After a while, I and a few others (whose names I do not recall) decided to try to reach our troops in Italy.

THE SECOND POLISH CORPS

We traveled to Italy on our own, principally by hitchhiking. I do not remember much of it, except that the American soldiers were amazed by our American World War I uniforms. We went through Brenner Pass right after the official cessation of military activities in Europe. We encountered the troops of the Polish Third Carpathian Division north of Bologna, who greeted us like long-lost children. We were given new summer uniforms and were settled in tents in a transit camp. We were fed the usual Polish-British army food. I remember especially the white bread, the orange marmalade, the weak sweet tea, and the instant powdered potatoes.

In this small transit camp most of us were former AK soldiers, but there were some western Poles who had been drafted into the German army and, luckily for them, sent to the western front. Apparently, the German High Command was afraid of pan-Slavic feelings among them. There were also a couple of young fellows, former slave workers in Germany, and, more important, at least for us AK fellows, former partisans who had recently escaped from Poland through the still-porous borders. They told us about the Communist government's persecution of former members of the AK.

It was then that I saw a photograph of the famous poster showing a heroic Polish soldier of the Communist government attacking an AK dwarf with the caption, "Reactionary Dwarf Covered with Spittle" (Zapluty Karzeł Reakcji). This poster was ubiquitous in "liberated" Poland. My brother Bronek told me later that for him it was the first concrete manifestation of the new regime in Poland.

The year 1945–46 was a time of intense debate among the former AK soldiers and the other soldiers of the Polish Second Corps in Italy concerning the return to Poland. The corps was originally organized in the USSR by the British and the Polish (London) governments. The soldiers were former inmates of the gulag or other Polish citizens forcibly removed by the Soviets into their territory during the Molotov-Ribbentrop friendship era (September 17, 1939–June 22, 1941). The British moved the whole army first to Iran, then to the Middle East, and finally to Italy. Polish soldiers were, of course, very anti-Soviet, or, more correctly, they were terrified of Soviet might. Many of them expected that sooner or later Western Europe would be overrun by the Soviets.

In the fall of 1945 each soldier received a letter signed by Aneurin Bevan, Labour Party foreign minister in the British government, saying that his government sincerely hoped that all the

Polish soldiers would decide to return to Poland. This letter stimulated further debates. The decision was more or less easy for those among us who had close relatives, especially wives and children, in Poland.

For the chaps like me who had gone through the AK Warsaw experience and whose parents were dead, the decision was difficult. It was further complicated by the news we received. We listened on the radio to the Polish government-in-exile, now no longer recognized by any real power. Their information about Poland (which later proved to be quite accurate) presented a bleak situation in the Polish People's Republic in general and the undisguised animosity toward the AK in particular.

General Okulicki, the last commander in chief of the AK, and fifteen others were arrested during their attempts to normalize relations between the new government and the AK and put on trial. That the trial took place in Moscow and that AK personalities were accused of—what else?—collaboration with the Nazis had a chilling effect on all of us, even the younger men who had initially planned to return to their families in Poland. The proceedings of the trial were broadcast in all European languages.

It is difficult to reconstruct my feelings about repatriation. The political aspects were clear enough. Radio Warsaw transmitted incessant anti-AK and, something that few people remember now, more and more open anti-West propaganda. In the shortwave broadcasts directed specifically at soldiers, the message was loud and clear: "Come back, your homeland awaits you." So far so good, but there invariably followed a statement clearly labeling us, the former AK people, criminals: "The amnesty has been proclaimed." It was the word *amnesty*, pronounced in the new, harsh, Stalinist tone, that more than anything else made the thought of returning home repugnant.

But as I examine my decision to remain in the West, I realize that that there were many other, personal factors. I learned officially from the Red Cross, sometime in the fall of 1945, that my mother and sister had indeed been killed in Ravensbrück. I had known this fact, but there must have existed a lingering hope against hope that they had survived. The official confirmation of their deaths put an end to all kinds of hopeful dreams. I fully realized a pure and simple fact: I was an orphan. I also learned that my aunt Janina and my uncle Kazik had survived. I loved them, and I remembered how selflessly and generously they had cared for me in the past. But I did not want to be a burden any longer. I knew that the material conditions of all Poles were bad and that the Warsaw survivors' condition was particularly so.

All that I have said so far is perfectly rational. But the decision not to go back, the feeling that I became conscious of in the freight train taking us across Germany in October 1944, was not, could not be, purely rational or even purely conscious. The memories of a less than friendly reception at the Bagniewskis at the beginning of the war, enhanced by my teenage sensitivities, stayed with me for a long time.

After meeting people of all nationalities in the camp, I came to consider my "Polishness" (beautifully translated, later, by my French-Canadian wife as *la poloniaiserie*, from *niaiserie*, "foolishness") as an insult of fate. I was, and have always remained, a patriot. The unexpected sight of a red and white flag has always stirred my emotions. But the object of these emotions, Mother Poland, stirred many other and contradictory feelings. Our generation of the AK was, of course, patriotic, but at the same time many of us were reluctant to express this patriotism in the traditional "romantic," emphatic language deeply ingrained in our culture. Many of us, including Franek and me, were ironic and even sarcastic in expressing our patriotic feelings.

Here is an example. Sometime during the second month of fighting in Mokotów, an officer of the prewar kind was teaching our wounded fellows how to respond properly to inquiries concerning their condition. If a superior officer asked, "Are you in pain?," the correct response was, "Yes, sir, but it is all for Mother Poland." But a simple young Warsaw guy, who was asked, "Do you suffer?," answered instead, "Yes, sir, it is all for Mother Poland, f*** her mother!" (To za tą Matkę Polskę kurwa jej mać!)

The simple fellow's answer immediately became known among all of us in Mokotów. It was repeated over and over as a wonderful joke. The success of this wisecrack stemmed from the fact that it was witty (two kinds of mothers) and that it mocked the official language of the army (a tradition of all armies). But, more important, it expressed the deep, contradictory feelings of many of us, feelings that were rarely verbalized. We were patriots hurt, in the very depth of our beings, by our patriotism. It took me a long time of living in North America to assuage these largely teenage feelings.

In the Polish army in Italy I was becoming increasingly aware of my love-hate relationship with my Polishness. It was impossible to discuss it with any of my friends. In fact, I was ashamed of it; it was treasonous. But I do not deny that this relationship with my country and its culture was one of the complex personal, psychological, and political reasons that, at the end of summer 1945, I decided not go back "there." I, of course, shared this decision with many of my comrades, but the reasons we discussed among ourselves were "reasonable" and expressed in political terms: "Who the hell wants to go back to the gulag?" (the term *gulag* was very well known among Polish Second Corps soldiers, long before Solzhenitsyn made it current in the West).

I wanted to learn English. Therefore, in the fall of 1945 I enrolled in the Signal Corps Officer Training School, which offered courses in math as well as English. The math training was good, but I did not learn much English. Instead, I learned it on my own with my Officer Training School friend Paul Itner (a Silesian and former member of the Wehrmacht). We took English lessons from a strange and strange-looking Italian polyglot. We paid him for his lessons, but I believe that he wanted to teach Polish soldiers in order to acquire knowledge of their challenging Slavic tongue. I learned enough English from him to continue studying on my own.

In the army school I enjoyed the nonmilitary studies, but I was irritated by all sorts of wishful thinking expressed by some of the officers. They insisted that the British were only pretending to be friends with Stalin and his atrocity-ridden regime. "Sooner or later we will liberate Poland," they would muse. I continued to study and wait for an opportunity to start life as a civilian.

Since I spoke French quite well, I thought of France. But the news from the French consulate in Rome was very discouraging.

The French did not wish to have any more "displaced persons." This lovely UN euphemism was referred to by its American abbreviation, DPs. I was in correspondence with my brother Franek, who was himself in France, in a Polish army establishment. Generally speaking, he was the opposite of an army optimist. He was finishing his high school education in an army-run school, and he was convinced that nobody in the West wanted Polish immigrants. Franek was far more bitter than I was.

For us, the former AK men, the regular army was a period of peace and quiet. There was a Verification Commission established for us. Until the commission's determination of our rank, we were considered privates. In 1945 the commission notified me officially of my rank: junior sergeant. This gave me a raise in pay and a bottle of Scotch once a month but otherwise caused me a lot of trouble. I still looked frightfully young, and the soldiers, other than the former AK men, were frankly shocked that such a young fellow was a junior sergeant when they, members of the army since 1942, were rarely similarly promoted. To avoid their unpleasantness, I tried not to wear my badges of rank. In the summer uniform it was easy, since the badges were removable.

I did not find army life easy or satisfactory. In 1946 the British organized the Resettlement Corps in Great Britain, and we were dreading the thought that we could be sent there. In England there was widespread animosity against the former "gallant allies." We became known as anti-Soviet and therefore Fascist troublemakers. I was waiting for an opportunity to leave Europe.

TO CANADA

The opportunity arrived in September 1946. The Canadian government offered to accept three thousand Polish soldiers from Italy to become farm laborers. Those who chose to do so would have to sign a contract with the Canadian Department of Agriculture stating that they would work on a farm for two years. Afterward they would receive their normal "landing papers"; that is, they would become regular immigrants. I, along with perhaps two other members of the Officer Training School, offered ourselves as candidates. We overruled the objections of our officers. A typical objection was, "Future officers of the Polish army should not plan to have careers as farmhands." Nevertheless, we participated in the Officer Training School graduation ceremony. It meant automatic promotion to the rank of full sergeant, which I needed like a hole in the head.

Immediately after the ceremony we went to another transit camp, near Naples, where Canadian officials selected the candidates. They wanted real country boys. And there were plenty to choose from. I would never had made it, except for the fact that I could communicate in English. Although I answered incorrectly the question, "What do you harvest first, oat or barley?," I was chosen because I did some translating for the Canadians.

After a few days we received temporary Canadian identity cards (mine was a low number, 382). After what seemed an interminable period of waiting in the transit camp, we finally embarked on a British Liberty ship and sailed to Halifax. At the moment of embarkation, I had a very bad case of the flu. I was the sole patient in the ship's small infirmary, where I was lovingly cared for by two Polish male nurses, who tried to prolong my stay as long as they could. But, unfortunately, I got well, and the ship's doctor ordered the unemployed nurses and me back to the general quarters. There were practically no officers on board, so the officers' quarters on the ship were given mostly to officer candidates like me. We were lodged in a relatively comfortable, large cabin. We spent the last period of our twelve-day voyage studying English like mad.

PART TWO

"WHITE"

The New Country

FIVE

Canada

We Polish soldiers who decided to work in Canada arrived at the port of Halifax on November 11, 1946, which was Armistice Day and Polish Independence Day. I was fully aware that this was a momentous change in my life. Many of us, conscious of this moment, kissed the ground. Some Canadian onlookers were obviously astonished by this outlandish activity. I forgot that I had kissed the ground at the wharf in Halifax until I saw Pope John Paul II doing it on television during his numerous foreign visits. It is an old and solemn Polish custom offering a respectful greeting to a new land.

After a short delay, we were divided into groups designated by the names of Canadian provinces. I was put into the "Alberta" group and given a white armband, this time to indicate that I was an interpreter. Now I understood why the Canadians had picked me despite my meager agricultural background: I was the only available translator in the Alberta group.

In the evening the whole Alberta group boarded the train. The big, old-fashioned passenger cars could be made into reasonably comfortable sleepers at night. Canadian soldiers on board cooked plentiful meals. All at once I became an important person, the only contact between the three hundred "Albertans" and the railroad and military authorities. Our trip lasted several days, with a lot of time waiting on spur lines. Obviously, our train did not have priority over the regular rail traffic.

I remember only two things about this trip. The first is the enthusiastic reception we got from the Polish Canadians who were waiting for us at various stations. One of the older members of a welcoming party was disappointed that we did not wear the traditional Polish uniform, especially the headgear, but were dressed like British (and, for that matter, Canadian) soldiers. I pointed out to him that we had badges saying "Poland" on our upper sleeves, but this did not satisfy him.

The second thing I remember is my initial impression of the country. There were friendly people at the stations and an occasional journalist or two. The latter struck me as profoundly ignorant of anything Polish. I remember speaking French with a young mounted policeman somewhere in Quebec.

After leaving Ontario, we traveled across the immense plain of southern Canada. It was during the first half of November, and there was snow on the ground. I was pleasantly impressed by the little towns and lonely farms punctuating the vast and cold landscape. But the majority of the people on the Alberta train were former prisoners or forced settlers in the Soviet Union. Several had a strange but understandable reaction to the landscape. I remember one country fellow who was genuinely distressed. "It's too vast, far too vast. It looks and feels like the Soviet Union," he muttered.

Finally, we arrived at our destination: Lethbridge, in southern Alberta. We were lodged in a few empty barracks next to a large camp for German POWs. The prisoners looked fit, well fed, and proud. In Lethbridge, we were officially separated from the British service. We got our separation papers, some separation money, and clothing allowances.

Our group began to disperse. I was taken, with some eighty others, I think, to Edmonton, capital of Alberta. As the only English speaker in the group, I was interviewed by a newspaperman. In a perfectly normal fashion, he asked me my name, but I immediately became suspicious. Reverting automatically to my *konspiracja* training, I gave him a false name. In fact, I was afraid that the Dembowskis in Poland might have difficulties with the Communists for having produced a "member of the AK reactionary forces."

The article duly appeared in the *Edmonton Journal,* and I was unable to explain to the Canadians why my name was printed "Solkowski." My English was not good enough to elucidate our *konspiracja* obsessions for the Canadians.

The first evening there was a dinner and a party for us, organized by the local Polonia, the Polish Canadian association. I was impressed by the obviously easy and friendly relations between the Polonia and the officials of the Ministry of Agriculture. I learned with astonishment that the employees of the government were called "civil servants." This kind of bureaucracy was previously unknown to me. The dinner party was my last Polish army occasion, for we were all civilians now.

During this dinner, or perhaps a little later during my occasional Sunday visits to Edmonton's Polish Roman Catholic parish, I met a friendly French Canadian, a minor civil servant. I remember only his last name, Lambert. I impressed him with my French. Later I met his family. His wife was a high school teacher who worked under her maiden name, Bessie Dunlop. Much later, at the University of British Columbia, I met one of her former students. He told me that she was a good, demanding teacher, nicknamed "Dunlop Tires." Unlike his Scottish Presbyterian wife, Mr. Lambert was a good Catholic, and something that I did not know existed until then: a Catholic patriot. He was an ardent supporter not only of other Catholics, but of all things Catholic.

At the time the relationship between Catholics and other Christians was more tense than it is now. At least there was a lot of anti-Catholic talk. Even in my presence, I heard a Protestant minister complaining that bringing the DPs to Canada was simply a Catholic plot to fill Canada with Catholics. The program had been organized by the prime minister, the Catholic Louis Saint-Laurent. Such loose talk provoked many Catholic reactions that were not necessarily healthy or sane.

But there was also a "patriotic" Catholic reaction, as exemplified by Mr. Lambert. The Lamberts helped me to see that there was much more to Canada than the work on the dairy farm. They, and especially Bessie, also encouraged me to study. During my two years in the Edmonton area, I was their frequent guest. I remain grateful for their friendship and moral support.

THE FARM

I had been afraid to write to Janina or her family from Italy. Being an ex-AK man and a member of the Polish army in Italy to boot was, in my mind, enough for the Soviet-style police to make trouble for my relatives. I wrote only when I was settled on the farm. And I wrote as if I had always lived in Canada.

Until the very end of the Communist era, we wrote our letters in a wartime *konspiracja* manner. For example, this is how Janina notified me that her sister Dzidka had gotten a six-year prison sentence: "She's moved to Mokotów, and she plans to stay there for at least six years." Mokotów was the site of Mokotowskie prison. Janina and my other relatives were surprised to receive my first letter from Alberta.

Before leaving for Canada, I wrote to Franek that I had signed the contract. I remember his suspicious DP reaction: "You will work for two years, and then they will send you back to Europe." The letters from Poland indicated that everybody was getting an education. This reinforced my own desire to study after I fulfilled my contract.

The day after that first dinner, I left for the farm. An official of the ministry, a Mr. Maundy, picked me up and drove me some sixteen miles west on the highway to Jasper. The contract I had signed stated that I was going to the farm of Mr. Melvin Jespersen at Spruce Grove. It was, if I remember correctly, late on Sunday afternoon when we arrived. Mr. Maundy presented me to a man who was milking cows in the barn and then left. The barn was lit by coal oil lanterns, and the milking machine compressor was driven by a gas engine. Since my outlook was still very Polish, I did not realize that the man I had just met was the owner of the farm and not a farmhand.

I was to spend the next twelve months in the Jespersen household working chiefly with the cows. Jespersen's Danish name hid his German origin. In fact, his family was old American Pennsylvania Dutch. His father had come to Alberta from the eastern United States in the early twentieth century because the Canadian government was granting free land in Alberta.

The most important thing about the Jespersens (there were two other brothers who were farmers nearby) was that they were very religious, fundamentalist Christians. To avoid theological disputes, the brothers had built their own church in the village of Spruce Grove and hired their own preacher. The congregation was small, consisting only of the Jespersen families and one or two old people from the village.

The very small village of Spruce Grove—two large grain elevators, a feed mill, a garage, and a small grocery store—had other Protestant churches too. There was also a very small Catholic chapel, with a nice old priest who served some other Catholic centers in the district. For serious shopping we had to go to Stony Plain, which was dominated by a large general store run by Sam Komisarov. I sent some cloth to Uncle Kazik that I had bought at Komisarov's.

On Sunday mornings I attended church services with the Jespersens, and if the time for Mass coincided with the Jespersens' services, I attended Mass. I was quickly learning all sorts of things about the religious situation in my new environment. I noticed that many of the fundamentalists I encountered believed all sorts of strange things about Catholics. Among other things, they thought Catholics were not Christians because they drank beer. On the other hand, the teetotaler Jespersen informed me very happily one day that his barley was good enough to be qualified for malt, that is, for beer and whiskey making.

The Jespersens did not like Jews "because they did not work with their hands." But there was only one Jew in the district, the above-mentioned Komisarov, whom they respected for his business acumen and honesty. Prejudices against the pope, popish power, and popish plots abounded among the Jespersens' coreligionists whom I encountered during my early days on the farm. The local priest knew his Protestant neighbors well and understood their prejudices. But he never expressed any negative judgments about them. "You are lucky. The Jespersens are good people," he often told me, and he was right.

Life with the Jespersens was rough, but only on one account: too much hard work. Two of us were taking care of about thirty-five milch cows, and there was a total of about fifty cows and one (dangerous!) bull to be fed. Feeding them was not much of a problem. The green feed and hay was stored above the cows. In the summer before my arrival, Jespersen's farm had been reclassified from "mixed" to dairy farm. That meant that he had to guarantee to produce a certain minimum quantity of milk every day. He acquired more cows and was slowly getting rid of his pigs. I was impressed that during the harsh Alberta winter the pigs did not live in the sty but outside hidden in an enormous pile of straw left expressly for them.

Life was quiet and friendly, but the days were long and hard. We got up at about five o'clock in the morning, and we started the day by milking the cows. Milking took place before breakfast and before supper. We had a milking machine system consisting of three units. The real difficulty for me was that every morning I had to start the small gas engine. The engine was capricious and responded with difficulty to the low temperature. Every morning was a struggle.

My work consisted of washing the cows' udders, an unpleasant thing for both the washer and the washees, because the soapy water in the pail quickly got cold. Then I had to change the belt, from which the milking unit was suspended, on each cow. Jespersen was always in charge of milking. I had to learn when each cow was finished and remove the milking unit at just the right time. The freshly gathered milk was put in the big, heavy collecting cans and immediately cooled in a large tank of water from the nearby stream. The milk, which had to be cooled but not frozen, was picked up by a dairy truck from Edmonton at about eight o'clock in the morning.

After milking, the real work of cleaning the barn began. Removing the manure produced by all our well-fed cows was the most strenuous daily exercise. We had no modern equipment, just a shovel, a wheelbarrow, and muscles. Jespersen helped me with shoveling and wheeling only on the days when he was in a hurry. Otherwise it was exclusively my job. Later, while traveling in America, I noticed that most dairy farms had barn-cleaning installations. A conveyer belt leading to a little elevated tower deposited the manure outside the barn in a neat mound. The machine bore the symbolic name "La Joie." How I regretted that we did not have such a machine on Jespersen's farm. I believe that La Joie was introduced several years after the war.

Breakfast, at about eight o'clock, was a gargantuan meal: porridge, bacon, countless eggs, countless pancakes, toast, and coffee or Postum. But I paid for it by enduring the lengthy, before-breakfast Bible reading and extended prayers pronounced by Jesperson. I remember once when my head was piously bent next to the sweet-smelling stack of pancakes, I had to use all my willpower not to bite into them. For my benefit, the readings and prayers were usually done in English, although Jespersen knew that I understood German better than English in those days.

Jespersen used to explain to me in German the English terms that I found difficult. I remember one of his explanations, which much later I quoted in my language classes. I asked him, "Boss, what is 'steady'?" He answered, "Steady, das ist aber shlow und shteady." He himself laughed at his "explanation."

The Jespersen family consisted of Melvin, his wife, and two adopted boys, Kenneth and Garry, aged twelve and thirteen. I know that the wife was a 1928 immigrant to Canada and that her family belonged to the German minority in Poland. She was reluctant to talk about it. It was her younger brother, a newly established farmer nearby, who talked to me about their family. As a very young child he had to attend a Polish school.

The Jespersens seldom talked about the war. He, of course, was exempt from military service because he was a full-time farmer. He was a loyal Canadian, and so was his wife. They did not wish to hear about my experiences during the war. And very early in our acquaintance Jespersen would repeat, "Wir müssen nicht über der alten Heimat schwertzen" (We must not chat about the old country). But they were conscious of their German background and sympathies. I could sometimes hear them praise the Germans for remaining loyal to their government to the end of the war.

My real friend on the farm was a dog named Rover. The sympathy was mutual. Rover followed me everywhere, and I talked to him in English to practice the language. He, unfortunately, did not speak.

The only people who gave me a bit of a hard time at first were the two boys. They teased me and indulged in all sorts of little chicaneries. Later, in the middle of winter, my situation with the boys improved because a neighbor's son came to me for help with a simple trigonometry problem. I helped him, but Jespersen was not pleased with this development. He told me that it confirmed his suspicions that his Polish farmhand worked better with the pencil than with the pitchfork.

I was not a good farmhand. It took me the whole winter to improve. I learned to drive an old tractor, with iron-spiked wheels rather than rubber tires. My monthly wages rose, from the minimum according to my contract, $45 a month (plus room and board), to $60 a month. During the harvest season, late September to the beginning of October, my wages rose to $8 a day.

I found the system used for threshing very interesting. Several farmers in the district collectively owned a steam engine, which powered the big threshing machine (also owned collectively, I believe). All the farmers worked together. The order in which their fields were to be worked was determined by drawing lots. I've often thought about these arrangements among the Alberta farmers. They worked well, they were voluntary, and, at least for the harvest period, they had all the character of a *kolkhoz* but without terror, without shooting, and without a gulag. In 1947 Jespersen must have drawn a late lot, because we were working on his harvest the last. We had to work far into the night, with the farmers' cars aiming their headlights at the threshing machine.

Right after the harvest, I met a neighboring farmer whose father had come from Poland. I still remember his name: Nizol. We chatted a bit, and he told me that he would be willing to sign my contract for the next twelve months though he did not need me, enabling me to go to Edmonton and work there.

And thus in November 1947 I became a free man. It just so happened that the afternoon that I was leaving the Jespersens, the official from the ministry came to inquire about me. I told him that I was leaving for Nizol's farm, and he took it very well. The Jespersens were quite glad to see me go. They liked me, but to them I was a "pencil man" not really fit for the life of a farmworker. They suspected that the Nizols' contract was a phony one, but like most Canadians they did not believe in labor contract arrangements organized by the state.

Looking back at my twelve-month stay with the Jespersens, I realize that it was an important period in my life. After all the physical and emotional experiences of my last seven years in Europe, hard physical work, excellent food, and stress-free human relations constituted a twelve-month retreat period for me. I became less nervous, more sure of myself, and more able to assume the position of a normal citizen. I am quite sure that the descendants and relatives of my boss, Melvin Jesperson, still farm in Spruce Grove, Alberta. I send my friendly greetings from afar.

EDMONTON

I found a small room in Edmonton with a Polish Ukrainian family whose name I have forgotten. Both Polish and Ukrainian were spoken in the home. The Polish members of the family, the wife and her sister, were Roman Catholics, and the Ukrainian members, the wife's brother-in-law and his family, belonged to the Orthodox Church. Though everybody spoke his or her own language, everybody was understood.

I paid only for my room, but soon the lady of the house let me use their kitchen, and I became a real member of the household. Her husband, a Polish meat cutter, had left her some time before. She was very distressed by the fatal illness of her younger son, who suffered from rheumatic fever, and in fact he died soon after my arrival. Her older son was a freshman at the University of Alberta in Edmonton, incredibly proud of himself, snooty toward me, and fully convinced that a "greenhorn" like me would never make it into the university.

My first order of business in Edmonton was to take care of my teeth. They were badly damaged by the wartime conditions. I had to spend a lot of money and several afternoons at the dentist's. He removed some of my back teeth. As soon as I recovered from the dentist's work, I began to look for a job.

The period from the middle of November to the end of December has always been a boom time in meatpacking houses. Extra workers, usually drawn from the ranks of farmers' sons, were hired as temporary help. I was immediately hired by Gainers Ltd. Many farmers' sons did not have a social security number, and I, of course, was in their group. One day we were dismissed early in the afternoon and told not to come to work without a social security card.

I was astonished that nobody in the governmental office asked me for my papers. I simply told the official that I was Peter F. Dembowski, born on December 23, 1925, in Poland, and he gave me my card five minutes later. Incidentally, that was how I became "Peter." I was gradually forgetting the officials I had dealt with in Europe, whether Polish *urzędnik* or German *Beamte*. This was indeed a new country!

As soon as I settled in Edmonton, I began to take night classes at Alberta College, an adult night school. I studied English and French grammar. The classes, like my relatives' letters from Poland, sharpened my desire to go to university. While I was still on the farm, Janina had sent me my Polish high school diploma, as well as my baptismal certificate, which took the place of my birth certificate. I had them translated into English by a friendly Polish parish priest. The high school diploma must have struck the Canadian university officials as strange. They would have had a hard time grasping that my high school was illegal under the German occupation. The certificate, issued by the Polish Verification Commission of the Ministry of Education, was based on an affidavit furnished by my chemistry teacher. He was one of my teachers who survived the war.

My work at Gainers Ltd. lasted until Christmas. After a short period of unemployment, I found a new job with the help of a new friend, a former Polish immigrant. My new job was in a big lumberyard, Berger Ltd. Their trucks had "Here Comes Berger" signs on the front and "There goes Berger" on the back. The signs were a good lesson to me; the distinctions between "come" and "go" and "here" and "there" are handled differently in Polish. The manager of that department of Berger Ltd. was M. Gagnon, a French Canadian, the second one after Lambert that I had met in my life. He was surprised and happy that I did not pronounce his name *gag-nun* like my colleagues but with a proper French accent. Two or three of his other workers were also French Canadians. They were pleasantly surprised that we could chat together *en français*.

The job at Berger Ltd. was important for me. It was the first job at which I was any good. Neither on the farm nor at Gainers was I a good employee, and this had given me a sense of failure. But my long hours at the Jespersens had improved my physical strength, and this made me a champion piler and handler of lumber. Soon I was promoted. I became a truck driver's helper and had an assurance from M. Gagnon that I was next in line to become a full-fledged delivery truck driver. By September 1948, when I was leaving Berger to go to the university, I could drive, and I already had a temporary truck driver's permit.

The established Polish immigrants were upset that I was leaving. They had my career all planned out for me. I was, in their minds, a capable fellow. Any greenhorn who after only eight months almost became a delivery truck driver was capable. According to them, I was to marry one of their (numerous) daughters, buy a plot of land, construct a properly winterized garage, move there with my bride, slowly build the rest of the house, and then live happily ever after as a capable employee of Berger Ltd.

I rejected this vision of security. Now, looking back at my long life, I realize that my decision to continue my studies was a crucial one. I owe this decision chiefly to the encouragement that I had always received from my family and from my teacher Wicher. In Janina Dembowska's family, learning and teaching were "natural" occupations. My family and my teacher instilled in me the unshakable idea that study is the proper, and perhaps the only, way of life.

During my early stay in Edmonton, I became a member of the Canadian Legion. The man who accepted my application was a Canadian veteran who, unlike the general public, knew all about the Second Polish Corps and even about the Warsaw Uprising. This membership helped me greatly when I attended university.

Finding a university that would take the risk of accepting a foreign student was a problem. I had had a bad experience when I was still at the Jespersens'. One Tuesday morning we went to Edmonton. (Farmers always go to town on Tuesdays. That is why the U.S. elections are held on Tuesday.) While Jespersen went shopping, I took the streetcar to the university. A sour-looking registrar, named Taylor, spoke to me for a few minutes. He probably doubted the validity of my high school diploma, and he was not impressed with my farmer's overalls. He was doubtless one of those fellows who regarded a Polish immigrant as poor student material.

In Edmonton there was quite a bit of prejudice against the large population of "Ukes" and "Polacks." We were lumped together as "bohunks" or "hunkies." Since the Edmonton area had no blacks and very few Jews, the people had only the bohunks and hunkies as the objects of their prejudice.

Anyway, the registrar, prejudiced or not, asked me a calculus question that I could not answer. He then told me that I could not be accepted at the University of Alberta. I was distressed because as a centralization-minded European, I believed Mr. Taylor's decision applied to all Canadian universities. But here my friend Bessie Lambert was particularly helpful: she set me straight, telling me to apply to the University of Saskatchewan and the University of British Columbia.

In the summer of 1948 I did apply, and, to my immense relief, I was accepted at both universities. I chose to go to the University of British Columbia (UBC), at Vancouver, because its acceptance letter came first.

UNIVERSITY OF BRITISH COLUMBIA

Acadia Camp

I left Edmonton by train in September 1948. After paying for my ticket, I had the colossal sum of $450 in my pocket. If I remember correctly, the UBC fee for the first semester was about $300. I was scared by this voyage into the unknown. I remember that I wore a rosary underneath my shirt. I arrived in Vancouver during registration week.

In 1948 the campus had a considerable number of former soldiers, who were supported by the Department of Veterans Affairs (DVA). The DVA students were running the show. At the Canadian Legion office, I talked to a chap who had served in Italy and knew all about the Poles in the British army. He told me that, as a veteran, I had priority in being accepted into university housing and getting service jobs. I applied at the university housing office.

I was accepted into Acadia Camp. About half of the students in Acadia Camp were army veterans. Room and board cost $45 a month. University housing and much of the rest of the rapidly enlarged campus consisted of former military camps constructed with standard army huts. Acadia Camp bore the name of its former military establishment. It had about thirty huts, each with a long corridor with rooms on both sides and with toilets and showers in the middle. A triple hut served as the kitchen and dining room. A boys' common room and a girls' common room were used for entertainment and social activities. In those prehistoric times it was altogether correct to call university women "girls" and men "boys." The camp was about 40 percent female and 60 percent male. I remember my first English linguistic joke: I insisted on calling the girls' common room, "common girls' room." Everybody corrected me patiently, not realizing that I was making the mistake on purpose.

I immediately got a job, washing dishes, or rather loading and unloading large dishwashing machine trays. I remember the culture shock of discovering the housework was not done by the residents for free, as had been the case at my old Bursa in Warsaw. Working about three hours a day (at suppertime) and receiving 70 cents an hour, I made more than $60 a month, the monthly maintenance payment for DVA students. Thanks to the Canadian Legion, my daily living expenses were thus assured in Acadia Camp.

Veterans were important to the university as a whole. The pre-war sleepy University of British Columbia, originally an offshoot of McGill University, suddenly received thousands of new, older, and usually better motivated students. The influx of veterans increased not only the quantity but also, I believe, the quality of the students.

In Acadia Camp I really blossomed. When I look at my situation there from the safe distance of years, I realize that it was there, perhaps a little tardily—I was twenty-two when I came to the university—that I began to lead the normal life of an ordinary young man. In Poland, my generation had become adults prematurely. In Acadia Camp I felt secure, which give me the feeling of equality with the people with whom I came in contact. I made many friends, especially among the veterans, most of whom were ahead of me in their studies. But I made many friends among the younger people too.

My first roommate was Ernie Payne, a very smart black man from Barbados. He introduced me to many other West Indians. They were a lively lot, very much divided between the islands and the mainland. I spent at least four Christmas recesses with the West Indians, when most of the other students went home. After a rum or two, I could even, or so I thought, sing calypso. One person in this group, Anthony Dummett, from Guyana, has remained a good friend. I was the best man at his marriage to a Canadian nurse.

In my second year I had another roommate, who was much more typical of the times. Stewart Smith was a former Royal Canadian Air Force man, a navigator on a mine-setting plane in the Pacific. He survived many dangerous missions—dangerous not so much because of the Japanese actions but because of the weather conditions, which were treacherous and constantly changing. Stewart was older than I was, and we got along very well. He married an Acadia Camp woman, also a former service person, named Margaret Nelson. Stewart and Margaret moved to the married quarters of Acadia Camp and had a baby girl, Susan. I baby-sat for her.

In Acadia Camp I became very friendly with the Wright sisters. The older one, Mimi, whom I met in the first year, was an intelligent, positive, and truly good-natured person, in addition to being neat and pretty. Her father, a prominent engineer in the smelting town of Trail in the interior of British Columbia (my joke, constantly corrected by my friends: "in the inferior of British Columbia"), was a sports fanatic and wished he had a son, a real athlete. He tried to make Mimi into the next best thing, and she was in fact an incredibly good basketball player. Unfortunately, her basketball coach had a strong anti-intellectual influence on her. I detested him because I was a little bit in love with her.

The next year her younger sister, Nancy, came to UBC. She was slightly disorganized and not very neat. She had a fine sense of humor, and musical talent. To simplify the situation somewhat: I was a little "interested" in Mimi, and Nancy was a little "interested" in me. More important, Mimi considered me Nancy's friend and therefore off-limits to her. Nothing romantic could come out of such a situation, but I acquired two good friends.

Later, my wife and I kept in touch with Nancy and her husband, Tony Antonacci, a musician with the Toronto Symphony Orchestra. We talked about our puppy love and "growing up" in Acadia.

Soon after arriving in Acadia Camp, I met two Polish students. The first was Leslie Adamkiewicz, a son of the prewar Polish consul in Ottawa. Although born in Poland, Leslie was educated in Canada. In 1939 the consul was convinced that there would be a lasting peace in Europe, and he sent his wife and two sons to Poland for the summer. He himself stayed in Canada. Leslie spent the German occupation in southern Poland, learning the art and science of making *bimber*, homemade booze, and surviving a period in an AK partisan detachment. Right after the war, he obtained traveling papers from the Canadian consul in Poland but for some *konspiracja* reason under the name Alexander. He came back to Canada legally and reverted to his Polish family name.

Like me, Leslie worked in the kitchen in Acadia Camp. He had a difficult temper, but I seemed to have a good influence on him. During one episode, he was supposedly threatening a young dietitian. As soon as I appeared he started to laugh, and the dietitian, apparently not very frightened, started to laugh too. Her name was Patricia, and she had been a British refugee child, sent to Canada in 1940. Leslie and Patricia were married after his graduation from the School of Agriculture. They lived in Ontario, near the town of Ayre, where Leslie acquired a good farm. He died young and unexpectedly; he apparently suffered from a heart condition.

The other Pole was also an interesting character. His name was Bill (Bolesław) Boreysza. He was an easterner, born and raised in the city of Vilna, and like many other easterners, he was an ardent Polish patriot. The Soviets occupied that territory in 1939, and soon after, they arrested Bill for his alleged resistance activities. The Soviet secret police considered him a far more important resister than he really was. He was interrogated for a long time and kept in solitary confinement even longer. Finally he was sent to a gulag, where he acquired a deep hatred not only of the Soviet Union but also of common criminals, who were treated as class-friendly allies of the prison administration. In late 1941, Bill learned about the recently declared "amnesty" for Polish citizens.

After many difficult trials, Bill joined the Polish army led by General Władysław Anders. Like the rest of "Anders' Army," he was sent to Iran. General Anders was not killed by the Soviets, as were thousands of other Polish officers, because he was being interrogated by the NKVD in Moscow, in the infamous Lubianka prison. He survived, precisely because he was suspected of anti-Soviet crimes during the Polish-Soviet war of 1920; only the unsuspected ones were killed.

Later, Bill went to the Officer Training School and fought in Italy. He was shot in the eye during a patrol. Somehow he survived the wound and returned to the base. He recovered, one of very few Allied soldiers who survived with a bullet lodged in the lower part of the brain. I do not remember how he came to Canada.

During his third year at UBC, Bill became ill with a disease that is rare in America, tuberculosis of the kidneys. The cure then was rest and quiet. He spent several months in Shaughnessy Military Hospital in Vancouver. I visited him there and remember the doctors' interest in his head wound. I had to defend him from a half-demented social worker (a recent graduate from UBC) who wanted to know all about his childhood and his relationship with his father. Bill told me that if she came to see him again he would maim her. I passed the message on with pleasure. Bill recovered and obtained a BA in Slavic studies. Later, he got a job at the Hoover Institution at Stanford University, where he became a good friend of Alexander Kerensky, the first post-czarist head of the Russian government, who was overthrown by the Bolsheviks. He became a good friend of our family at Berkeley during my PhD studies there, but we subsequently lost touch with him. He told my wife a lot of things about his horrible life in the Soviet Union.

Extracurricular Activities

Looking back on my adaptation to university life, I realize that it was the first place where I felt at home after many years of being an outsider. Naturally, I took full advantage of the rich extracurricular life at UBC. Because I had friends who were members, I became active in the Visual Arts Club. As in Edmonton, many professors were traditionally anti-Catholic. The "official" reason: Catholics were undemocratic; priests told them how to think and how to vote. Professor Andrews, assistant to the president and a real power on the campus, with whom I became quite friendly, told me once that "the Catholics always vote the way the bishops tell them to." At first I did not fully grasp the point he was making, but later I was struck that this liberal man believed what he said.

My main intellectual and political activity was fighting with friends of the Soviets. There were many kinds. The first, most general and most manipulated kind were members or followers of the World Peace Movement. This Moscow-sponsored organization was very popular at UBC, simply because it stood for peace. For me, the methods used by the movement were like Leninist tactics. I was once invited to a party at a local Protestant church. I received the invitation from Dorothy Fox, a student and the daughter of a British naval officer and a White Russian woman. Dorothy spoke some Russian, and I was struck by her considerable feminine charms. She became the wife of an Australian fellow traveler, John, about whom I shall speak later.

The party, which I eagerly attended on account of Dorothy, turned out to be a Moscow appeal-signing session. I walked out disgusted, and disappointed in my charming Dorothy. I was learning fast. The appeal for peace was one of the well-orchestrated political movements of the 1940s and early 1950s. Many people who signed the appeal were, of course, not Communists at all. But all the arguments for peace were based on the premise that capitalists in general and the Americans in particular were warmongers. The World Peace Movement flourished until the USSR got its own atomic bomb.

The second kind was composed of a small group of actual Communists. It was led by a young veteran who was well versed in Leninist dialectics and tactics. The Communists usually did not organize specifically Communist meetings themselves but in a Front populaire fashion; that is, meetings were organized by various sympathetic groups.

Once, in about 1949, there was a huge noon hour meeting to listen to Hewlett Johnson, the "Red Dean of Canterbury." The biggest lecture hall on campus was filled to overflowing with people eager to listen to this important spokesman for the World Peace Movement. His speech was not about peace but the heroism, beauties, and virtues of the Soviet people. Although it was not difficult to speak about the Soviet Union's heroism during the Great Patriotic War, his speech contained countless idiotic, emotionally charged anecdotes from his travels in the Soviet Union. I was eagerly waiting for the end of the speech to ask the dean a question. I finally got a chance to ask him in Russian, "Do you speak Russian, Father?"

The Red Dean did not answer; instead he raised his head and started to pray. But the chairman of the meeting, head of the local Stalinists, whispered something to him. The dean answered my question: "Former Polish soldiers who are now in Canada are all former Nazis. Most of them served in the SS!" I was stunned and absolutely speechless, a condition rare for me. Most of the audience seemed to believe the dean. I felt a chill around me.

A good example of a fellow traveler of that era was the man mentioned above, John. He was an Australian supported by an annuity left to him by his deceased father. For some reason he liked me, despite my "reactionary" politics. We met while washing dishes together. He did not need the money, but he wanted to associate with the "working class." He was intelligent and capable of thinking clearly about all sorts of things, except the Soviet Union and the United States. When I first met him, I talked to him about eastern Poland, the transplantation of the population, gulags, mass murders, and so on. His reaction was simply, "Are you trying to tell me that all the political idealism of the Great October Revolution has been lost?"

Like many others of his ilk, his love of the Soviet Union was counterbalanced by a boundless hatred of the United States. Unlike the Red Dean, one of a number of the British intelligentsia who had become Tolstoyans in early age and then transformed their Christian Tolstoyism into a love of Russia and, later, of the Soviet Union, John had none of the Tolstoyan mysticism, but he fully shared the antiestablishment disposition of this group. John's philo-Sovietism was probably based on hatred of his own "capitalistic" background. He kept secret the fact that he had an assured income from his father; he mentioned it to me in a moment of weakness. Right after the war he came to Canada with his mother, spent a few months of unruly service in the Canadian army, and "fell in hate" with the United States.

An egoist above all, John was, politically speaking, a loner. He did not join the Communist Party, probably because the Party required discipline. But he was a Leninist at heart. He was with me at the Red Dean's lecture. He knew very well that there were no former SS men in the Polish forces, only young soldiers drafted into the Wehrmacht from western Poland who declared their Polish nationality once they had been captured by the Allies. But John completely approved the Leninist principle followed by the Red Dean: Do not argue with your adversary; instead, attach the badge of infamy to him.

John's mother believed that I had a good influence on her son, but she was quite wrong about this. Nobody could have much influence on this passionately self-centered and ideologically obsessed man. I knew vaguely that John later became an academic geographer in Britain. Many years later, in Chicago, I met a British geographer who, rara avis, was not a left-winger, and I asked him whether he knew a geographer with John's name. He said, "Yes, I do. He teaches in Africa, and he is just about as Red and unreasonable as most of the British geographers." John has never gotten in touch with me and vice versa.

In a way, I'm glad to have met John. He prepared me to face the student revolt in the late 1960s when I was dean of students at the University of Chicago. In his behavior, his capriciousness, and his self-centeredness he was an early precursor of the rebellious students of those later times.

Left-wingers, Stalin worshippers, and Lenin lovers were not the only closed-minded people at UBC. The School of Social Work, founded right after the war, was run along strictly orthodox Freudian lines. An Austrian war refugee encouraged the school to accept Freudian principles as dogma. I do not believe that there was much opposition inside the school to Freudian thought, but there certainly was opposition outside the school, for example, in the Department of Psychology.

The various Marxists and the orthodox Freudians had many characteristics in common. They were both fascinated by "Theory." They did not really analyze a given situation in social or personal life; rather, they isolated those elements in a situation that "explain" it in the light of a preconceived ideological stance. Both of those groups were fanatics, often unaware of their fanaticism. They believed that they were "progressive" and "scientific," or perhaps better, they believed that those who disagreed with them were "reactionary" and "antiscientific."

Summer Jobs

An important part of student life at UBC was summer employment. The long summer break invented by the canny Scots allowed the willing student to earn enough (or almost enough) money to live through the winter. My first summer job ended very quickly. The campus employment office found me a helper's job in a roofing company. I lost this job after two days. We worked on a tall office building downtown, and the foreman immediately noticed my fear of heights. I was fired.

I went back to the employment office and got a job in a gold mine that was situated in the interior of British Columbia and accessible only by railroad. The large mine was in a small mountain locality called Bralorne. I went there with my roommate Ernie Payne. The pay was good, and we worked eight-hour shifts. We were lodged in comfortable barracks, and we ate in a restaurant open twenty-four hours a day. Not being claustrophobic, I liked working in the mine. We newly hired miners, the temporary helpers, were called "muckers."

What we mined was quartz, which contained gold. To my disappointment, I never saw a gold nugget. The mined quartz was thrown into a system of chutes in order to break it into smaller bits. From there, it was brought up to the surface to be crushed further. The crushed quartz was, I believe, shipped away to have the gold extracted from it.

Upon returning to university in my sophomore year, I began to look for my next summer job. I found it through a former employee of Chipman Ltd. of Winnepeg. The job consisted of servicing the chemical spraying train on the vast railroad network in western Canada. All the tracks that were used to haul grain and lumber had to be kept relatively free of the weeds that grew like mad on these secondary lines. Chipman had a contract for weed control with both the Canadian National and Canadian Pacific Railroads.

The Chipman crew, three of us, worked with the train crew responsible for the given section of track. We mixed the chemical agent with water and sprayed the tracks. One man stationed on each side of a bench on the car saw to it that his side of the spraying apparatus was working correctly. Behind the locomotive was our chemical tank car and two cabooses, one for the train crew and the other for us, the chemical crew. I either invented or passed on the formula to begin the spraying: "Let us spray!"

What I particularly liked about the job was that we did not work in rainy weather and we had no travel priority. Therefore, we spent a lot of time sitting on side tracks or waiting in a small town for the new railroad crew. I loved the job with its long waiting periods and occasional frantic hurry to get ready to work.

In my second summer working for Chipman I was promoted to the position of foreman of the chemical crew. I made the error of giving the helper's job to John. He was often a sullen and rebellious worker. His ceaseless preaching of "revolution" to the railroad people brought us a visit from the Royal Canadian Mounted Police (RMCP) in a small place near Prince Rupert. The Mountie explained to me that he had received a notice that there was a wild Limey revolutionary (John) and his Russian companion (me). He was an intelligent fellow, so I was able to explain John's idiosyncrasies as well as my non-Communist Polishness to him without too much trouble.

Working for Chipman Ltd. for three summers was a real piece of good luck. I saved quite a bit of money, and I really liked the job. It gave me a chance to get to know the backcountry, usually unseen by tourists.

One cultural experience will always stay in my mind. We were waiting for a spraying mission somewhere in south-central Alberta, spending the weekend in a small, predominantly Native village. On Friday night a film was being shown in the church hall. Everybody, including us three Chipman men, went. It was an old-fashioned cowboys-and-Indians film. What was illuminating was the spectators' reactions: they were completely on the Indians' side. Every time a cowboy was shot off his horse, there was a loud, prolonged cheer. After a while, we realized that we should join the majority, so we too cheered for the Indians.

Studies

My studies, of course, were the main part of my life at UBC. During the school year I threw myself headlong into academic work. At first, my biggest problem was English. I took all the obligatory freshman courses in the first year, including mathematics, which I found quite easy after the Signal Corps Officer Training School classes. Otherwise, I planned to take chiefly humanities courses. UBC operated on the so-called Scottish system of two semesters a year. Final exams took place in mid-December and at the end of April.

To my great surprise, I passed all the December exams, including the freshman writing class. This convinced me that I could become a good student and that I should stay in the university. I borrowed a little money to pay the second semester fees. In my second year I decided to concentrate on foreign languages: German, Russian, and, above all, French. It was then that I became a good student, and I eventually received some scholarships.

I met a number of distinguished scholars at UBC. The first was a professor of classics and linguistics from Holland, Willem de Groot. He came to UBC under a cloud. During the German occupation, he accepted the position of dean of faculties in Groningen, I believe. After the war he was under investigation by the Anti-Collaboration Committee and decided to choose voluntary exile over possible public humiliation. UBC took him without question. It was later established that his conduct as a dean had been honorable and had resulted in the preservation of many cultural institutions and the survival of several endangered persons. He was completely rehabilitated but I think only posthumously. A new university building at his Dutch institution was named in his honor.

As a student I did not know all those things, but I learned about them when I myself became a university teacher.

I took a course in linguistics from Professor de Groot, who introduced me to the modern Prague school of linguistics. Most important, he became a model for me of the modern teacher-scholar.

The second important scholar I met at UBC was William John Rose, a specialist in Polish history and one of the most interesting persons I have ever met. He was former head of the London School of Slavonic Studies. He was a Canadian from Manitoba. A very pious Protestant, he became something like a lay missionary under the auspices of the YMCA early in life. In about 1912 he went to Polish Silesia, the Opole district, then under Austrian administration. He began to work there and, above all, learn Polish. I think that he had chosen the Opole district because there were a lot of Polish-speaking Protestants there.

When the 1914 war broke out, he was sent, with the other British subjects and politically suspicious members of the local population, to an internment camp. World War I internment camps were not the hellholes of World War II, and he took advantage of being there by acquiring a good knowledge of Polish from the interned Poles. All his life, Rose spoke Polish with a distinct Silesian accent.

Rose became interested in Cieszkowski, an original nineteenth-century religious thinker, who, although Catholic, was Rose's "soul brother." In the camp he wrote his first book on a Polish subject, *The Desire of All Nations, Being an English Edition (Abridged) of August Cieszkowski's "Our Father."* It was published in London in 1919.

I took several courses with Rose, the most important of which was a history of Central European nationalisms. Like de Groot, Rose became a role model for me. His wife died in about 1954, and Rose died in 1968, when I was already in Chicago.

Both de Groot and Rose were the beneficiaries of UBC's drive to hire established scholars from Europe. The university took advantage of the difficult situation of scholars, both Germans and DPs. Bringing in German scholars was an original and daring idea, for most of the Western world still regarded all Germans as Nazis.

The man behind the effort to engage good midlevel specialists like de Groot and Rose—the stars were snapped up immediately, by both the USSR and the United States—was an energetic physics professor of German Canadian background named Schrum.

I particularly remember one relatively young professor of physics brought to UBC by Schrum. His name was Kämpferer. I do not know why we became friends, but we did. He lived in married faculty quarters, consisting of army huts, like Acadia Camp. He was about five years my senior and had an interesting story to tell. He was a subaltern officer in the Wehrmacht. In the summer of 1942 his regiment was preparing to go to the Volga front when he became ill with polio. He recovered but became crippled; he walked with utmost difficulty. But, he told me, polio saved his life. His regiment was decimated at Stalingrad, and all the officers were either killed or captured, but the young Kämpferer went back to study physics in one of the best institutes in western Germany. Because of his strange army career and because he had not participated in the horrors of the final months of the war, he kept a clear head about the war. He certainly did not consider me a "hereditary enemy." We spoke about the war, comparing notes while enjoying our common Canadian residence.

Another professor fished out of Europe by Schrum was a Polish mathematician and physicist, Władysław Opęchowski. He left Poland voluntarily in about 1935 because he was opposed to the Polish government. He obtained a teaching position in a Dutch university and spent the war in Holland. But during the last months of the German occupation, he was sent to a concentration camp. He was married and had a teenage daughter, Sylvia.

These foreign professors (for even the solid Canadian-born William Rose was very British in outlook) convinced me that I should begin graduate studies. In 1952 I graduated from UBC with honors in French and Russian. That summer, while riding the Chipman train for the last time, I applied to the French *attaché culturel* in Ottawa for a scholarship for Canadian students. Since I had not registered in 1946 at the Polish Communist embassy in Ottawa, I was probably stateless, for those who did not register automatically lost their Polish citizenship. Professor Andrews, who knew everybody, arranged for me to receive Canadian citizenship individually from a judge rather than wait for the usual turn of the bureaucratic wheel.

The year 1952 was the time of the Korean War and a Red Scare in Canada. There was a police investigation of my citizenship application. An RCMP corporal came to see me in my Acadia Camp room in the spring. We spent a few minutes in idle conversation, and finally he asked me an ominous question: "You don't have any [Communist] ideas, do you?" I answered, "No sir, I don't." I received my citizenship in a brief swearing-in ceremony in the downtown office of the judge. I shall always be grateful to Canada for this favor.

During the summer I received a positive answer to my application for a French government scholarship. It covered room and board in Paris for one year, as well as tuition at the Sorbonne.

S I X

Paris, Marriage, London

PARIS

In the early fall of 1952 I made arrangements to travel to Paris. A room in the Fondation Canadienne, at the Cité Universitaire, was reserved for me. I bought a Halifax–Le Havre ticket on an old Cunard ship called *Carinthia*, perhaps a confiscated German ship, and traveled to New York with my friends who drove their car.

In New York I said good-bye to my traveling companions and took the boat train to Halifax. The *Carinthia* was full of students, and the sea voyage was pleasant. I arrived in Paris about eleven o'clock at night and took a taxi to la Maison Canadienne.

The next morning, I met my roommate, a French student from the Albi region in the South of France. His name was Gérard Charmasson. Like many descendants of the Albigenses, he was a Protestant. Later, he invited me to come home with him for the Easter vacation. His pleasant family consisted of a grandfather, grandmother, father and mother, and one sister. Since I was always interested in linguistic habits, I found the Charmassons fascinating. The grandparents spoke Provençal (Occitan), the parents a very local French, and the children Parisian. Somewhat like the Polish Ukrainian household in Edmonton, everyone spoke in his or her own language but was understood by the others.

From the beginning of my stay in Paris, I was serious about my studies. I registered in a formal course designed for future teachers of French. It bore a majestic name: Cours de Préparation et de Perfectionnement des Professeurs du Français à l'Étranger. This was an intensive course of writing, vocabulary building, and pronunciation. Pronunciation was combined with an introduction to general phonetics and was taught by the personnel of the Institut de Phonétique, the oldest European institute of its kind, founded at the end of the eighteenth century to teach the deaf.

The director of the Institute spoke with the thick Catalan accent of his hometown, Pau, in the Pyrenees. He gave excellent lectures on general phonetics, but it was Mme Léon, his assistant, whom he called upon to offer examples of proper French pronunciation. Later, the same Mme Léon became my colleague in Toronto. The Cours de Préparation had several outstanding teachers. I learned a lot about French, and about language teaching in general, from them.

I was also an *auditeur libre* in several courses. I attended the Russian-language courses at the Institut des Langues Orientales ("Langues O," in the student dialect). The course was crowded, and I did not learn much, but I met several Algerian students who were studying Turkish because they admired the great Atatürk. History did not go their way. They were passionately anti-French and saw the world through the optics of that passion.

I was very busy and also very poor. The French government scholarship was quite meager. At noon, I ate in a Jewish student restaurant that served kosher but bad food; in the evening, at the Cité Universitaire cafeteria.

Soon I began to start work on my thesis. I got the main idea for it from de Groot. The Russian language uses Church Slavonic vocabulary as a source of "learned" words. There is a superficial parallel between the Latin vocabulary introduced to the Romance languages in the course of their history and the Church Slavonic vocabulary introduced by Russian speakers when they needed to express a somewhat more abstract idea. I wanted to base my thesis on purely phonetic and nonsemantic criteria and found a professor who reluctantly agreed to be my thesis director after reading my proposal. He was not a linguist but a well-known historian of Russian culture, Pierre Pascal. Students liked him, and knowing that he was a Catholic, they called him *père Pascal*.

Much later, I learned his story from François Furet's book about the "recovered" Leninists, *The Passing of an Illusion* (Chicago, 1999). Pascal was one of the first Christian thinkers converted to an unbounded affection for Mother Russia. In 1917 he transferred this affection to the revolution in general and to Lenin in particular. As a Frenchman who knew Russian, he was at the time part of the French Mission in St. Petersburg, but he refused to return to France, choosing to work for Lenin instead. The French court charged him in absentia with desertion.

Pascal was one of the first French converts to Leninism, but as an honest, moral thinker, he was one of the first who realized the illusory nature of Communism. In fact, he abandoned his Communist involvement even before the death of Lenin. Later he returned to France, where his desertion charges were dropped, and in due course he wrote a thesis (on a Russian religious rebel of the seventeenth century) and became a professor of Russian at the Sorbonne. I met with him only a few times. He could not advise me on linguistic matters, but I found a young French lecturer who knew what I was driving at. He encouraged me greatly.

Pierre Pascal made a very good impression on me. Unlike many other academics, he did not disapprove of my unwillingness to return to my Polish *patrie* to lend a hand to the construction of socialism. So many of the academics I met in Paris were Party members, fellow travelers, or at least vociferous sympathizers. Pascal never mentioned his views to me, but I knew that he was free from those leftist ties. And like de Groot and Rose, Pascal was a true scholar.

In the second year of my stay in Paris I did not have a fellowship, but the French made me an *étudiant patronné du Gouvernement*, which gave me some small but important privileges. I borrowed $480 dollars from UBC and managed to live on it for the next twelve months. In order to reduce the costs of transportation,

I bought a cheap old bicycle whose pedal shift had to be welded every few weeks. I rode my bike between the Cité Universitaire and the Bibliothèque Nationale (BN).

I spent the summer of 1953 in the BN reading D. N. Ushakov's multivolume Russian dictionary, using it to find terms whose phonetic characteristics pointed to their Church Slavonic origin. For several weeks I read nothing but the Russian dictionary, and my persistence won the hearts of many of the elderly, shabby, and regular BN patrons. At that time, well before the reform of admission procedures, the library was full of semihomeless, semi-*clochard*, older people with some pretenses to engaging in intellectual activity. They had probably obtained their *cartes de lecteur* at a time in their lives when they had had a legitimate need of the library's resources. But in 1953 what most of them sought in the BN was a roof over their heads, light, a certain amount of heat in winter, and the comfort of other maniacal colleagues.

I finished the collection of index cards in early fall and began to write my thesis. I worked on it chiefly in the Bibliothèque Slave, near the Sorbonne. The library was poorly heated, and I wore all the clothes that I possessed. The winter of 1953–54 was one of the coldest in Paris history.

I become a good friend with *gospodin* Boutchik, the chief librarian. I remember his wit. The first time I went to the Bibliothèque Slave I arrived armed with a letter from my thesis director and a brief memorized speech in Russian. I tried to speak with the best Russian pronunciation I could. He thanked me kindly in the purest St. Petersburg accent and told me that he was going to register me as a reader and wrote my *carte de lecteur* in his calligraphic hand. In the meantime he gave me something to read, the latest issue of *Gazeta Polska*. So much for my good Russian pronunciation.

I had worked out the theoretical basis of my dissertation in a graduation essay I had written under de Groot for UBC. There were still many important theoretical problems to be worked out in the thesis, but there were some purely practical ones as well. In 1954 typing in two alphabets was complicated. The final text was typed in French first, leaving the exact number of spaces for the

Russian words. Then I rented a Russian typewriter with spacing similar to the French one, and another typist (who knew Russian) insesrted the missing Russian words. I typed these memoirs on a simple Macintosh computer. All I have to do is open the Moskva font to type a Russian word.

After many struggles, in the summer of 1954 I finished my thesis and also wrote the two required complementary essays. One was on the three hundredth anniversary of the "reunification" of Russia and Ukraine, as celebrated in the USSR in 1953. I discovered and discussed many documents published by the Soviet Academy on this occasion. The collection was falsified, chiefly by omissions: Polish documents were simply not published. The other essay was on the Polish poet Julian Tuwim, who had recently died. I published a modified English version of this essay in 1955; it was my first academic publication. During the public defense of my thesis, most of the discussion centered on the two essays, which had been read by two outside examiners. I defended my thesis at the end of June 1954, about three days before my wedding.

YOLANDE JESSOP

The most important part of my two years in Paris was not the diploma from the Cours de Préparation or the *doctorat de l'Université de Paris* but meeting Yolande Mariette Jessop, my future wife. She arrived in Paris from Quebec on September 8, 1953. There was a little group of people who wanted to make a trip to Holland and Germany by car. The car's owner, Willy Wilner, was an archetypal New York businessman. Like many other New Yorkers, he did not know how to drive. The driver was a young French Canadian musician, André Demers. He invited me to come along on the trip on account of my German. André told Willy that we needed another passenger in order to reduce the cost of gasoline for each of us. So he asked us to wait for a young French Canadian woman, who was to arrive the next day.

My first impression of this young woman was most favorable. She was tall, smiling, and dressed in an elegant brownish-green suit, which I learned later she had made herself. André introduced her to us as Yolande Jessop, originally from Rimouski and now residing in Quebec City. Just before coming to France, she had earned an MA in philosophy and French literature from the Université Laval.

Willy's car was a rather small English Morris. The driver, Yolande, and I sat in the front, and Willy and his friend, a silly girl from New York, sat in the back. The girl spent most of the trip worrying that her suitcase had fallen from the roof rack. Her worries were constantly rekindled by Willy, who from time to time said, "Oops! I saw something slipping from the roof."

I was sitting next to Yolande, and we began to talk. I discovered that she knew everything about the *psychoméchanique* (or *psychosystématique*) *du langage*. It was a linguistic theory and a language-investigating method recently developed by a French linguist, Gustave Guillaume. At Université Laval, Yolande was a student of Guillaume's only foreign disciple, Roch Vallin. I had learned all about Guillaume's theories from de Groot.

As soon as I heard that Yolande was conversant with Guillaumisme, I asked her to marry me. The question was half serious and half in jest. Yolande said yes, doubtless in the same spirit. For more than sixty years we argued about the exact time of that fateful question. Yolande said that I popped the question a full fifteen minutes after our acquaintance; I have always maintained that it was after only seven minutes.

A word about Yolande's background. She came from a mixed English–French Canadian family. Her father, James Jessop, was basically English-speaking but bilingual. He was an important lawyer and married a French Canadian, Léonie Gauvin. He died young in 1938. Yolande's mother died in the 1970s. The couple had four children, Albert, Jean-Marc, Yvon, and Yolande. Albert and Jean-Marc became lawyers. Yvon, the artist in the family, died quite young, Jean-Marc a little later. Albert died in June 2013 in Quebec. All the family was fundamentally French, but all, like Yolande, learned English. They were good Québecois patriots but not nationalists. Yolande's French became our family's everyday language.

The purpose of our trip to Holland and Germany was not only tourism. All of us, except Willy and his friend, were preparing to spend the winter in Europe, and we had heard that clothes were much cheaper in Holland. I had already started working inside the very cold Bibliothèque Slave, and I knew I needed a heavy turtleneck sweater very badly. During our long-running conversation, Yolande mentioned that she knitted sweaters for her gigantic brother, Albert, because he could not buy sweaters with long enough sleeves. I told her about my desire for a sweater, and she immediately suggested that she knit one for me from Dutch wool. I realized at once that her previous "yes" was perhaps not as playful as it had appeared at first. Indeed, we bought some wool in Amsterdam, and Yolande knitted me a heavy turtleneck, which I wore every day during that glacial winter of 1953–54.

After leaving Holland we went to Germany and traveled along the Rhine River. One evening we stopped in the little town of Bacharach, a commercial center for white Rhine wine. We arrived on the first day of Oktoberfest. New white wine was being sold cheaply in quarter liter glasses. I was thirsty and immediately consumed about four glasses. I found Yolande and, *in vino veritas*, began a long, somewhat repetitive confession of my love. She, apparently having drunk less than I, accepted these "openings of my heart" in an indulgent but friendly way. From the Bacharach evening on, we knew that our relationship was serious. We were both twenty-eight, old enough to be serious about our common future.

Back in Paris, Yolande found a tiny *chambre de bonne* on the sixth floor of an apartment building on the rue du Bac. Her landlady was a quintessential French *chipie*: she hated everybody (with the possible exception of the German occupation army), but above all she had a boundless contempt and hatred for anything American, including their *chouin gom* (1950s French for "chewing gum").

I was working like mad on my thesis, but in the evenings I visited Yolande on the rue du Bac. She had a couple of plates and glasses and just one kitchen appliance, a coffee maker. I discovered a method of making excellent *nouilles au gruyère* in the coffee pot. The trick was to add some cold water as soon as the water with the noodles started to boil over. Since the butter, cheese, and pasta bought in one of those little shops near the rue du Bac were excellent, my culinary invention was very appealing to Yolande. As for me, the meager cuisine of student restaurants had given me an excellent appetite. I found my *nouilles au gruyère* à la cafetière simply divine.

While still in Quebec, Yolande had purchased a small car, a Renault Quatre Chevaux, to be picked up in Paris. A word of explanation: France was recovering well economically (thanks in part to the Marshall Plan), but in 1953 the French needed to export their cars, so a French person had to wait months to acquire one. A foreigner could get a car immediately, however, provided he paid in hard currency. After a year the car could be resold for francs. Neither Yolande nor I had a driver's license, but I became Yolande's car-rental agent. Several Canadians and my new roommate, a young French postdoc MD, rented the car for an appropriate fee.

Yolande bought the Renault for a long-planned trip to Spain and North Africa with three of her Canadian friends. They left on December 10, 1953, and did not return until the second half of January. Yolande told me that it was a *beau voyage*; according to one of her friends, she spoke quite a bit about her *pauvre Pierre*. Before Yolande left Paris, she and I had an understanding that we would consider ourselves engaged. I was very happy to see Yolande back at the rue du Bac. That winter and spring we spent a lot of evenings together.

An important event marked the spring of 1954. Yolande became seriously ill with infectious hepatitis, which she had apparently contracted in the Cité Universitaire swimming pool. She was feeling quite out of sorts when I, faithful to the Polish wartime doctrine that a good meal can cure anything, invited her to a rue de Seine potato joint, a favorite place for hungry students, and bought her a big plate of deep-fried potatoes with deep-fried eggs. That did the trick: the next morning Yolande was in the Cité Universitaire hospital.

The new director of la Maison Canadienne, M. Lemay, a professor of chemistry from the Université de Montréal, made all the arrangements, and he soon became our good friend. Yolande spent several days in the hospital. She came out of the hospital thin and weak and had to go to a *maison de repos* at Bénodet in Brittany. While she was there, she wrote me amusing letters about her fellow patients. Soon after Yolande's return to Paris, she moved to la Maison Canadienne and set the date for our wedding. It was June 29, 1954, the feast of St. Peter, which is, according to Polish tradition, my name day.

THE WEDDING

Our wedding took place three days after I defended my thesis. Yolande took care of the preparations. We did not broadcast our intentions, but we did tell the very *sympathique* M. Lemay about our plans. Yolande absolutely refused to marry me in my old navy blue suit, which I had received as a parting gift from the army in November 1946. She found a tailor and had a fine new suit made for me. Of course, she paid for it, because I did not have any money. She also bought our wedding rings, inscribed *Y. et P. 29 juin 1954*. Yolande's witness was a very nice French Canadian lawyer from Montreal, Paul Crépeau, and mine was my cousin Paweł Matuszewski, who came to Paris from London for the occasion.

Just before our wedding, on June 26 or 27, I received a letter from Yolande's mother. The letter was formal, and the sentence (written in French) that stood out was, "I formally forbid you to marry my daughter." I was dismayed, of course. In my mind the wedding was also supposed to be a joining of both families. But Yolande took it less seriously. "Ah," she said, *"maman* got up on the wrong foot that morning." In fact, on June 28 we received a telegram from her with a money order of $100 for each of us, with a blessing for *"ses enfants."*

We later learned that she had held a family council with Albert and Jean-Marc and announced, "Your foolish sister wishes to marry somebody in Paris." Apparently they answered, "It's about time. Yolande is twenty-eight years old." My mother-in-law had a change of heart, hence her telegram.

She knew quite a bit about me, because Georges Jessop, Yolande's paternal uncle, came to Paris in the late spring of 1954 to, as he said later, "investigate" me. He had to leave before our wedding, but he seems to have given me a clean bill of health. He liked the company of young people and was in turn very popular with everybody in la Maison Canadienne. He was called "huncle," because that was how Yolande once pronounced his name. Until his death in 1984, *l'oncle* Georges was our great friend. He often stopped to visit us in Vancouver, Berkeley, Toronto, and Chicago on his way to his winter place in Puerto Vallarta, Mexico, more often after he retired from his management position at the Banque Nationale Canadienne in Winnipeg. He helped us with a down payment for our first house in Vancouver and left some money to his beloved niece Yolande in his will. He taught me a lot about how to be an old man.

On June 28, Yolande and I went to the British Consulate and had a brief civil marriage ceremony. A French law passed in 1903, during the anticlerical era, stipulated that a religious wedding ceremony could be performed only after the civil (legal) wedding. Unlike the U.S. Consulate services, which represent the civil law of the District of Columbia, Canadian consuls have no civil jurisdiction; therefore the British performed the ceremony. I remember that Yolande "the spinster" and Peter "the bachelor" were nervous and not very fluent in English during the brief ceremony.

The news of our wedding could no longer be kept secret at la Maison Canadienne. Receiving demands for a celebration, that night Yolande bought about $60 worth of *vin mousseux*, cheap bubbly white wine that cost less than a dollar a bottle, and we had a large drinking party attended by the residents of la Maison, augmented by the usual number of party crashers, many from the nearby Fondation Arménienne. I remember that at about ten o'clock, one of the Armenians asked me what was the occasion for the celebration. I said that a fellow was marrying somebody. His reaction was, "Poor wretch."

At the party we announced that the real wedding, that is, the Mass and the religious ceremony, would take place at eight o'clock the following morning, as we had arranged with *l'abbé* Joly. Many of our friends had obviously abused the freely flowing *vin mousseux*. I know that Paweł certainly did, for he was buttonholing the guests and offering samples of his jokes. After a while his question, "Would you like to be told a joke?," was met with an energetic "No!"

But hangover or not, everyone came to the ceremony, including our Jewish friends Gordon Adaskin and Jules Lebow and the Greek Orthodox Bill Filipiuk and many other nonchurchgoers. At that time, before Vatican II, a fast was observed before taking communion, so the Mass was held early in the morning. Filipiuk was charged with taking the collection, and he made sure that everyone obliged.

The wedding Mass was beautifully conducted by *l'abbé* Joly. Paul Crépeaux and my cousin Paweł (Paul) were the official witnesses. Crépeaux read the prescribed biblical passages so well that *l'abbé* told him after the ceremony, "Monsieur, you read like a professional." I met up with Paul in Montreal in the late 1980s. He had married a Frenchwoman and had become a professor of jurisprudence at the Université de Montréal. He spoke as beautifully and as mellifluously in Montreal as at our wedding. Paweł Matuszewski died in London sometime after our meeting.

After the ceremony, we went back to la Maison Canadienne, where M. Lemay had arranged for a simple but elegant reception brunch for us and our witnesses. Mme Leroy had lost the authority she wielded during the absence of the regular director and before the arrival of M. Leroy. She shed the traditional—but in her case crocodile—tears at our reception.

Yolande and I honeymooned at the charming hostelry Auberge de Quatre Sonnets in Saint-Rémi-lès-Chevreuse. After about six days, Yolande realized that we did not have enough cash with us to pay the bill, and I had to go back to la Maison Canadienne to borrow some money.

By marrying Yolande I entered the world of the French language not only as the language of my profession but also as a normal, daily medium. My wife and my children have always spoken

French at home. If we use English it is for jokes, for jokes always translate badly. Our grandchildren are for the most part monolingual; they have adopted the main language of the country, English.

LONDON

Yolande and I returned to la Maison Canadienne. Mme Leroy arranged for us to have a double room. We now had to make plans for the future. I did not have any prospects for a teaching job for the 1954–55 academic year because I had defended my thesis too late to apply anywhere. Yolande did not want to return to Quebec without my having a job there. We decided to go to London, where as Canadians, that is, British subjects, we could work. In France, we would need a work permit, which was practically impossible to obtain. We had visited London before our wedding, and we both liked John's mother, Wendy, who lived there.

In August we moved to London. We got a bed-sitting room in Golders Green, where foreigners were, apparently, tolerated better than elsewhere in London. Yolande made the room quite comfortable by buying a few things. I began my London stay by getting what our landlady called "a touch of a chill in the stomach." I spent three or four days in bed, quite convinced that I was going to die.

I did not die, and as soon I recovered, I went to an office of the labor exchange and got a job at Wall's, a meatpacking plant. My fellow workers were exclusively Irish or Polish. The official at the labor exchange told me that I would feel better among "my own kind." Only the foremen were English; they wore bowler hats to prove their national and work status. The work at Wall's was less strenuous than that at Gainers in Edmonton, but the pay was low: about seven pounds a week after taxes. I remember the absurdity of the British income tax system in those days. If you worked a couple of hours of overtime, you received less money at the end of the week because you had moved into a higher tax bracket.

SEVEN

Back to Canada

We were settling in for a longish stay in London. Yolande interviewed at the French Section of the BBC and received a job offer. Unexpectedly, I received a telegram from the University of British Columbia offering me a job teaching French and Russian as of September 15. I went to a travel bureau and booked passage from London to Hoboken, New Jersey, at the cheapest fare available. A very British ticket agent told me, "Don't worry, you will get there," and we did.

On the ship I had a bunk in a large dormitory cabin for men, and Yolande shared a three-bunk cabin with five other women. Most of my fellow passengers were Irish emigrants, giving me a taste of a fundamental American experience. Once we arrived in Hoboken, a kind customs officer told us that there was a flat rate for a taxi ride from Hoboken to Grand Central Station in New York. In the taxi I realized that after two years of not using English, I was a little rusty. But the taxi driver said, "Whatsa matta with you? Your English is poifec!" I felt somewhat reassured.

We took a train the next morning, and twenty-four hours later we arrived in Quebec, tired and happy. We had exactly 46 cents with us; we went to an early Sunday Mass and gave it all to the church. I met my mother-in-law and her two older sons and their family. Yvon, the youngest son, was not in town. I quickly got a favorable impression of both Albert and his wife, Paule Garneau, as well as of Jean-Marc and his fiancée, Emma Cova. Albert had received a quintessential French Canadian college education. He liked to erect and defend philosophical systems. When we discussed my reactions to Quebec's strict and formalistic observance of the Catholic religion, he said, "Mais tu parles comme un protestant" (But you speak like a Protestant). Jean-Marc, who was especially attached to Yolande, was more practical-minded.

Yolande and I kept our zero finances a secret, but my mother-in-law guessed. She did not talk about it, but I knew that she phoned all her numerous friends and told them that since we were leaving for Vancouver very soon and we had a lot of baggage, all our wedding gifts had to be strictly in cash. It certainly worked. By Tuesday night we had enough money to pay for our Quebec-Vancouver tickets and settle down in our new place.

UBC

I was very happy to have gotten a teaching job in two departments, French and Russian. I was promised a salary of $3,000 a year, paid from the budgets of the two departments. Of course, I knew everybody at UBC and was happy to be back at my alma mater.

Soon after my arrival I met the chairman of the Department of Slavonic Studies, an Australian. I believe that he had learned his Russian, which was perfect, at home. I admired his polyglot abilities and his fascination with languages but not much else.

I was to teach three elementary French courses and three weekly sessions in reading the Cyrillic alphabet. That came to eighteen hours a week. After about two weeks of classes, I met with the Slavic chairman again. He asked me, "How much are they going to pay you?" I answered, "$3,000," whereupon he said, "Let's see what I can do about that." I went home and told Yolande that I expected an increase in my salary. Instead, a few days later I got a letter from the administration telling me that my salary had been "adjusted" to $2,400 a year. Apparently the chairman wanted to save $300 of his departmental budget (paid entirely by the Ford Foundation), so he cut $600 dollars from my salary, and the French department did not protest. I was both enraged and humiliated. At that moment I decided that we should leave UBC at the earliest opportunity, but I kept this decision to myself. In fact, we left UBC two years later, in the summer of 1956.

Meanwhile, I was learning how to teach large French classes and, above all, how to control unruly students. Life in the faculty section of Acadia Camp was very pleasant. We had several friends, the professors I mentioned before and a young Englishman who taught English, Ron Baker. We also became friends with James Nyman, a blind man from the interior of British Columbia who was just finishing his BA. Yolande organized our little apartment and began to give private French lessons.

L'oncle Georges came to see us early in 1955. After a few days, he decided that we should purchase a house. He gave us $3,000 (or rather lent us, for I signed a promissory note to be paid on demand) for a down payment. We found a house near the golf course that separated the university from the city. It faced a forest that belonged to a Native reservation. We finished a room in the basement and rented it out.

ANNA

Soon after we settled in Vancouver, Yolande became pregnant. This first pregnancy was not easy, and she was often sick. Our eldest daughter, Anne Yolande, was born on June 16, 1955. She has never used her second name, and when she was about twenty-five, she decided to call herself Anna, for, she said, "tout le monde s'appelle Anne" (all the world is named Anne).

Anna was baptized in our parish church in Vancouver. She was a serious and quiet baby and was obviously very intelligent, but it took her a long time to walk and talk. Later, in Berkeley, the orthopedic doctor told us that she would need special corrective shoes, which had to be changed every two months or so. All I can remember is the horrendous price: $14 a pair. As a young child, Anna was quite withdrawn and spent most of her time alone, thinking.

Later Anna became a good but rebellious student at the University of Chicago high school. She graduated from Cornell College in Iowa, then specialized in computer studies at Loyola University of Chicago. For many years now she has worked in the computer department at the University of Chicago. She owns an apartment close to me and visits every night to chat with me. She takes care of her old father like the wonderful daughter she is.

DECISION

Not only was I upset about the salary matter "settled" by the chairman of the Slavic department, but I felt that the general atmosphere at UBC was less interesting than in my student days. De Groot, Rose, and Opęchowski were still there, but the student veterans were gone and with them much of the atmosphere of intellectual seriousness and excitement. There were many fine undergraduate teachers at UBC, hardworking and intelligent, but generally speaking, they were not scholarly minded. Most of my UBC friends promised me a nice quiet teaching career in French, if not in Russian.

The Slavic department became bigger but not better. By 1955 it could be described as comprising more or less two equal groups: White Russians and Red Americans. The latter considered themselves victims of McCarthyism. These two groups had nothing in common except a real antipathy toward Poles: *Poliachishki von!* (Out with the Polacks!) was their common, if usually silent, guiding principle.

This shared antipathy was based on different points of view. The White Russians objected to my Polish accent, which is indeed unpleasant to the Russian ear. It is a curious fact that Russians encourage non-Slavs to learn Russian, and they do not mind their foreign accent, but any accent other than Russian in a "brother Slav" is anathema. This is probably a pan-Slavic reaction, based on their considering all Slavs "potentially" Russian. The Red Americans (whose Russian was usually worse than mine) objected vehemently to my being anti-Soviet, therefore "fascist."

In the French department I met at least three former doctoral students from the University of California, Berkeley: David Niederauer, Ralph Boldner, and Pierre Robert. If not great scholars themselves, they knew what scholarship was. They talked about their former professors in terms of their scholarly achievements. Robert, a Frenchman from Aix-en-Provence, convinced me, without too much opposition on my part, that I should apply to Berkeley's Department of Romance Languages and Literatures for admission to the PhD program and, of course, a teaching assistantship. And UBC helped me make up my mind: my salary of $2,400 a year was $300 less than the salary of a teaching assistant at Berkeley.

I was, needless to say, a little afraid of Yolande's reaction to this move into the unknown. We were well settled in Vancouver: we had a house, a daughter, a smart cat. What more do you need in life? It is very pleasant to recall now that Yolande completely shared my view that although UBC was more or less comfortable, it was an academic dead end for me.

Looking back, I realize that I made two crucial decisions in my professional life. The first was to enroll in the PhD program at Berkeley in 1956. The second was to accept the offer of a position at the University of Chicago in 1966. I made both decisions despite having at the time relative professional and material security. Yolande fully supported and encouraged me in both decisions. I am forever grateful to her.

EIGHT

Back to School

BERKELEY

My application to Berkeley's French department was accepted, and in the late summer of 1956, I arrived first in Berkeley and rented a small backyard cottage for us. It was about a mile and a half from the French department on campus. Yolande arrived by train a few days later with Anna, the cat, and our humble possessions. Since we were unsure of the future, we rented out our Vancouver house. The rent was about the same as the mortgage payments. To simplify my travel to campus, we purchased a bicycle. The next summer we were able to move to a comfortable apartment closer to campus. We had to buy a washing machine on credit. I remember that the salesman, who was certainly used to dealing with poor graduate students, installed our machine and asked Yolande if she wanted try it. She answered that she had no soap and would have to wait until the end of the month (I was paid monthly) to buy some. The salesman went to his car and brought her two samples of detergent. The machine worked fine.

The washing machine was important to us because by then Yolande was expecting another child. It was also important because it helped us become good friends with our next-door neighbors, the Hsi family, Chinese refugees. The Hsis did not have a washing machine, and Yolande invited them to use ours. After each wash, Mr. Hsi brought over a big bowl of excellent Chinese food, saying, "Dear Mrs. Dembowski, I cooked a little too much for us. I hope that you can help us with this food." That gentle comedy lasted as long as we shared the second floor of the apartment house. We loved Mr. Hsi's cooking and counted on it.

About a year before leaving Berkeley, we moved for the third time. Although poor, we managed quite well. Yolande was a very good housekeeper and manager—she kept a booklet and recorded every cent spent—and she was doing more and more French tutoring. Every Berkeley undergraduate had to take at least four semesters of a foreign language. Yolande's specialty was tutoring the Hong Kong students in French 2. By the end of our stay in Berkeley, in the spring of 1960, we had saved enough money to buy a secondhand car. The car was a 1952 Plymouth with prominent fins. The idea was to use the car to transport our family to my new, and presumably permanent, job. My truck driving in Edmonton served me well. After a few practice drives with my colleagues, I passed the driving test with no trouble and obtained a driver's license.

EVE

The most important event of our four-year stint at Berkeley, besides my PhD studies, was the birth of our second daughter. We wanted to have children, and we could not wait until I had a good job. I was almost thirty-three and Yolande was thirty two when our second child was born, on November 28, 1957. This was Thanksgiving Day, and we have indeed been thankful for the gift of our daughter. She was baptized Eve Marie in an Oakland parish close to the hospital.

Yolande's second pregnancy was a lot easier than the first but still rather hard. She lost some forty pounds. She was well taken care of by the doctors in the Kaiser Permanente Foundation Hospital in Oakland, and the birth itself was easier. However, the doctors insisted that her relatively recent hepatitis and our incompatible

Rh factor would make a third successful pregnancy unlikely. During Yolande's short stay in the hospital I took care of Anna. It was a difficult job, because she sensed that something important was happening, and she cried and cried. But when Yolande came back home, Anna was very happy to have "la sœur Eve."

Much later, Eve finished her studies at Berkley Music School in Boston. There she met the star of the institution, Frank Strangio, an Italian American with relatives in Australia. Eve married Frank in Australia in 1980, and they have four children: Sebastian, born in 1983; Gabriel, in 1989; Sophie, in 1985; and Juliette, in 1994. We both went to Australia twice, and Yolande went there alone several times. In our old age, Eve visits me in Chicago. Like Anna, she is a wonderful daughter.

PHD STUDIES

The organization of the big Department of Romance Languages and Literatures was based on the principle that the teaching assistants (TAs) were teachers in the lower division (first two years of college) and at the same time graduate students. In my time at Berkeley, there were no graduate students who were not TAs. The system required a large number of TAs. This in turn meant that the TAs could scarcely manage to get through the strenuous PhD program. The average TA stayed about two or three years, got an MA, and left. The TAs were guaranteed four years' assistantship. There were some people who did an ABD, "all but dissertation," in four years, wrote the dissertation elsewhere, and received their degree later, but many simply disappeared. I remember only two students who received the PhD after four years: Karl Uitti and me.

The PhD program involved a lot of work, which in practical terms meant a capacity for assiduity. The Germans have an apt expression for this capacity, *Sitzfleisch*, which means "perseverance" (lit., "using your sitting flesh"). Since we all had to prepare the German reading examination, we certainly knew the expression. And the popular saying among the harassed TAs was that "without the *Sitzfleisch*, you cannot make it." I have always had the *Sitzfleisch*.

Since our small home was a domain controlled by our two energetic babies, I learned very quickly to study at the library. I have kept that habit to this day.

The first obstacle for the PhD students was the foreign language reading exams. German was a universal graduate student requirement. On top of it, the Romance languages department required Latin, French, Italian, and Spanish. The formal translation examinations were given at the beginning of each semester. I remember that in the first week of my studies I passed German, French, and Italian. The hard blow was failing Latin. I passed it at the beginning of the next year. In my free time I read old volumes of the Madrid journal *ABC*, from the beginning of the Spanish Civil War to its end. I learned to read Spanish well enough to pass the exam, but I also acquired political insight into Spanish history. In 1936 the journal was vaguely leftist but independent; by the end of 1938 it was a Stalinist rag.

Passing all the foreign language examinations made one an official candidate for the qualifying examinations. Those were oral examinations in French, Italian, and Spanish histories of literature. Candidates majoring in French, Spanish, and Italian were given reading lists of classical works. A lot of humor revolved around the existence of the reading lists. When I asked a witty colleague from the Deep South, Tom Watson, whether he had read Joseph Conrad's *Lord Jim*, he answered "No, it's not on the reading list."

The preparation for the qualifying examinations was the main preoccupation of serious students. By "serious," I mean those who believed that they would be able to finish their PhD at Berkeley. Preparation for the qualifying exams took different forms. I read the Italian and Spanish works on the reading list and sat in on the upper division college Spanish and Italian courses. In these survey courses I met outstanding professors, such as Diego Catalan de Menendez Pidal in Spanish and Aldo Scaglione in Italian. We also had many sessions of questioning each other and checking our file cards. I believe that I still have a small index card box with notes on the Spanish and Spanish American reading list. The box bears an apt title: *Todas las cosas y algo mas* (Everything and Something More).

In addition to teaching, we were obliged to take, for credit, two graduate courses each semester, each usually demanding a term paper. The professor I remember best was Yakov Malkiel, who gave a general course in basic problems of Romance historical linguistics. Although he was not much appreciated by his colleagues (not to mention many of his students), I fell under his spell. For me, he was *un vrai maître*, and he remained so all his life. Although an awkward and difficult teacher, he was well respected in his field and the founder and editor of the journal *Romance Philology*. As soon as I finished my PhD, he asked me to submit a short article about the special vocabulary of Robert de Clari, the subject of my dissertation. He also asked me to write innumerable book reviews, which is an excellent postdoctoral method of keeping up in one's field of study. His initial invitations were an important factor in my professional development. Malkiel convinced me that I could, in fact, become a scholar. In this, he helped me more than any other professor. He was a difficult character, though. He made enemies easily, and he kept some grudges indefinitely.

As a young boy, before the Russian Revolution, Malkiel belonged to the Jewish aristocratic milieu of Kiev and inherited a profound attachment to the Russian empire and to the Russian language, as well as a profound respect for German *Wissenshaft*. After the revolution he lived in Berlin, where he became a perfect German student. He always bragged that he was the best essay writer in his German high school. His scholarly virtues (and vices) were German.

I remained Malkiel's friend until his death in 1998, probably because I lived far away from Berkeley and had no chance to quarrel with him. It was difficult for many English-speaking professors to submit their texts to Malkiel's corrections. This was not my case: I accepted without complaint his sometimes painful style full of *préstamos*, *cultismos*, and *malkielismos* (borrowings, learned words, and Malkielisms). And thus I was the only former student of his who spoke at his memorial service at Berkeley.

I also studied with an Old French specialist with a truly medieval name, Percival B. Fay. Most of the students took his course on Old French texts because there was no paper to write and no final exam. Since he used the same texts year after year, many students had a "pony," that is, a set of translations into modern French of the texts that Fay used. But my friend Uitti and I decided to really learn Old French, and we prepared each class without a pony. Learning to read Old French was an important step for me in choosing my specialty. Fay was a perfect specialist, trained at the first center for Romance philology in the United States, at Johns Hopkins. He also introduced me to the art and science of textual editing.

A visiting professor from University of Michigan, Edward B. Ham, was even more influential in that area. He offered three of us—Uitti, a student named Kimball, and me—a practical course in editing. We studied in great detail photostats of the manuscripts of an early *Bestiare* written by Philippe de Thaon. We concentrated on textual problems. Ham was a learned but level-headed textual critic, and on top of it a pleasant and helpful teacher. He died rather young, long before his retirement.

The other Berkeleyan who become important in my intellectual life was Ronald N. Walpole, chair of the department. He was a Welshman and a member of the Turpin study and edition group in Britain. He was knowledgeable and enthusiastic and did good scientific work, especially after his retirement. He agreed to be my thesis director and took his charge seriously. Like Malkiel, he used to correct my written French and was in fact responsible for many French "infelicities" later found in my published text.

There were many other professors, and—what is rare in most universities—all, or almost all, were competent. There was a visiting British linguist (formerly a German refugee), Manfred Sandmann, who really encouraged me. There was also the philosophically inclined French "universalist" Francis J. Carmody. His medieval connections were strong, since he was the editor of Brunetto Latini's *Li livres dou trésor.* Carmody was a member of my dissertation committee and helped me greatly to define the scope and range of my stylistic investigations. I learned at Berkeley many practical aspects of what real scholarship should be. If not every teacher at Berkeley was an outstanding scholar, they all knew what scholarship meant. And that is the greatest compliment that I can offer here to my real intellectual alma mater.

I passed my qualifying oral exam one Saturday morning late in the spring of 1959. *L'oncle* Georges came to visit us, on the way from Puerto Vallarta, for this important occasion. He celebrated my examination in a big way—by handing me the promissory note for the down payment on our Vancouver house, with the instruction to burn it. I had more than a year to write my dissertation. I threw myself immediately into the work.

KARL UITTI

Karl Uitti and I met as soon as I became a student at Berkeley. He noticed me because I had passed three language exams (he had passed all five). He had studied at Berkeley for his MA in comparative literature and knew all the "ways and means" of being a TA at the University of California. Both his maternal and paternal grandparents were born in Finland. Karl was born in 1933 in an ethnic and staunchly Lutheran community in the Upper Peninsula of Michigan. Later, we met his extended family. After getting his MA, Karl left for France to teach English in a lycée in Nancy. He studied there and, later, in Bordeaux. In 1954 he was drafted into the army. This was during the Korean War. Having passed his army tests with excellent results, he could choose his place of service. He chose Germany in order, he told me later, to prepare for the German language exam for his PhD. He was a careful planner.

While in France Karl married a Puerto Rican woman, María, from New York. She was handsome and lively, but when we met her at Berkeley, it was increasingly evident that she was becoming "difficult." She also had a mean streak and soon developed an antipathy to Yolande and the rest of our family. She died sometime in the 1990s. The Uittis had two children, Emi (Maria Elisabeth) and Coco (Karl Gerard). Coco, a handsome boy, inherited his mother's mental troubles and died young. Emi is a fine woman who works in Spanish radio broadcasting in the eastern United States. I saw her and her husband at her father's funeral.

When I look at my friendship with Uitti from the distance of more than a half century, I realize that it was based on shared interests and passions. Both of us were absolutely convinced that we wanted to receive PhDs and become serious academics. We encouraged each other, and he, an old California hand, guided my first steps at Berkeley. We shared an admiration for Yakov Malkiel. We were both serious Christians. In addition to our shared professional interests, we liked each other's company. Karl got a job at Princeton and remained there to the end of his working life. At Princeton he became a friend of the French medievalist Alfred Foulet and trained himself to become Foulet's replacement. Karl became an outstanding medievalist.

We remained friends with him and his second wife, Michelle (Freeman). They have two sons, David Charles and Jacob Christian. But in about 1990 our friendship began to become strained, mostly because of his drinking. Doubtless, he inherited this penchant from his father, who, Karl told me, died at forty-nine of ethyl alcohol poisoning. Karl managed to work in spite of his drinking, and he managed to keep his secret from everyone except his closest colleagues. We preserved our friendship by staying away from each other, but unfortunately I was called upon to take part in an intervention organized by his friends in Princeton.

Karl recovered, more or less, but the experience of the intervention weighed heavily on our minds. We met several times afterward, we traveled together, and we attended AA meetings together, but the friendship was not what it used to be. Karl died in November 2003. He was not quite seventy years old. His was an exemplary Christian death. Surrounded by his family and visited by his pastor, he died soon after the communal recitation of the Our Father. I attended his funeral. To this day I feel distressed by his death, but at the same time I recognize my debt to this incredibly gifted and intelligent man. He profoundly influenced my intellectual and professional life.

PHD AND JOB SEARCH

Immediately after passing the qualifying exams I started working on my dissertation. Even before the exam, I had discussed my dissertation topic with Walpole. Through my undergraduate studies with de Groot and my Parisian *doctorat d'université*, I had become a language-centered student of literature, in older terminology, a "philologically minded" student of literature. I have remained so throughout my professional life.

For the dissertation topic, I chose to analyze the language and style of the earliest known Old French chronicle, written at the beginning of the thirteenth century by a simple Picard chevalier, Robert de Clari. It was one the first chronicles written in Old French, or rather in a quite pure Picard dialect, and, most important, it was written in prose. It is probably difficult for a nonspecialist to imagine that in Old French a verse form was used long before they "discovered" prose. Walpole was the director of my dissertation, and Malkiel and Carmody were first and second readers. It took me at least fourteen months to produce the dissertation.

Of course, I was writing in the BX (Before Xerox) and BC (Before Computer) eras. The former came to Toronto the year we arrived there. In order to have a text with large margins, I bought two copies of the Clari edition and pasted both sides of each page in a large copy book. My dissertation was written in French, corrected and typed by Yolande. Eve was smart enough to be born at the end of 1957, and the tax deduction we received for her for the whole of 1957 was enough to buy a good Olivetti manual typewriter.

My PhD advisers, Carmody on style and Malkiel on linguistics, were very helpful, but Walpole, as director, was perhaps less so. There was another problem: my committee members were not on speaking terms with each other. I had to be quite diplomatic when speaking about one committee member's reactions to my work to another member. I took a little vengeance on them. In the printed version of my dissertation, I wrote a dedication to my committee members that consisted of a paraphrase of Robert de Clari to the effect that "tot sunt molt preudon et molt boin clerc" (all [three] of them are very wise and very good clerks).

During our last months in Berkeley, I worked very hard on my dissertation, and, as always, I taught two classes, each five times a week. We had left our apartment and were living in the Berkeley hills, in a beautiful house belonging to a Swiss professor named Meylan, who asked us to house-sit for him while he was visiting Switzerland. He came back in July but allowed us to continue living in his house. I wrote and corrected several pages of my text every day, and Yolande typed those pages at night. Meylan admired our industry and advised Yolande to take a hot bath after the night's work so she that could take care of her daughters next day. His advice proved to be helpful. Meylan suffered from old man's diabetes, and he insisted that red wine is a natural remedy. I remembered his insistence later, when I myself was diagnosed with "senile" diabetes. I faithfully drink some of this remedy each evening with Anna.

In order to receive my degree in the summer session of 1960, the approved and cleanly retyped dissertation had be deposited in the administration building no later than five o'clock in the afternoon of August 1. I still remember my joy at turning in my dissertation at four o'clock that day. Our car was packed with all our humble possessions, and Eve and Anne, very excited, were waiting for me in the backseat. We left Berkeley immediately. Thus ended my long student career: I was almost thirty-five years old.

My academic success is largely owed to my wife, Yolande. She encouraged me at every step. Her confidence in my abilities increased my own confidence, so necessary in the long drive toward a PhD. She also helped me immensely by correcting my students' papers, a time-consuming operation. Her assistance gave me more time for my studies. But, above all, she encouraged me because she had complete faith in my abilities, which gave me strength to proceed.

During the last five months or so of writing the dissertation, I started to look for a job. Here Walpole was very helpful. He wrote to several institutions on my behalf, and I got three bites: Yale, Michigan, and, later, Toronto. In those days there were practically no advertisements for jobs. It was done in an old-fashioned way, chiefly by the old boys' (and old girls') network. I wrote a long letter to Yale, explaining my unusual background, and the chair there, a learned and noble Frenchman, Henri Peyre, replied. He said that the beginning jobs at Yale were usually two-year assistant professor stints, never leading to tenure. Nicely but firmly, he told me that I was a family man and thus too old for this temporary job.

Next I corresponded with the University of Michigan. I got the job, but the financial authorities could not approve the appointment. The university was in one of those, mostly political, budget crises and was financed with funds from the veterans department. There was, of course, a temporary freeze on hiring.

Walpole wrote to the chairman of the French department at Toronto University College, Dana Rouillard, a splendid and patient Yankee of Huguenot origin. His department offered me an assistant professor position. I accepted, although as a student in Vancouver, I had heard some strange hyper-British stories about Toronto. I must add that 1960 was a good year for getting an academic job. Universities were expecting a boom in the student population, and many of them, like Toronto, were beefing up faculty in expectation of the future shortage.

NINE

University of Toronto

Our little family traveled to Toronto in the Plymouth. It took a long time, because in 1960 there were no interstate highways. We traveled on two-lane roads, stopping in parks with swimming pools at noon so the girls could play.

I was well received by my colleagues at University College, but I was surprised to find that the university had hired another medievalist, a fellow I knew from la Maison Canadienne in Paris, John Flinn. He was a veteran of the Canadian army and had spent many years at the Maison Canadienne. Flinn wrote a very good dissertation on the *Roman de Renard*, which was published later by the University of Toronto Press.

Hiring two medievalists at the same time was the first indication that Toronto did not share Berkeley's attitudes concerning the importance of specialization and of stressing the common teaching-scholarship endeavor. But I was happy to have a real job. My Berkeley dissertation was published by the University of Toronto Press in 1963 (*La Chronique de Robert de Clari: Étude de la langue et du style*), and I immediately started to work on my first editorial project, the chanson de geste *Jourdain de Blaye*.

After a while, I realized that I was temperamentally ill-suited to the spirit of Toronto. It was basically a good undergraduate institution founded in the mid-nineteenth century on a series of compromises. The original departments, whose purpose was to train preachers, were English, French, Classics, and Oriental languages; these constituted the so-called college subjects. They were taught in independent colleges: Victoria College (United Church), Trinity College (Anglican), St. Michael College (Catholic), and University College (nonreligious, run by the university itself). All other university subjects, such as science, history, Spanish, and so on, were outside the purview of the colleges.

Each college had to teach the same courses, and the detailed content of each course had to be the same every time. But each college had the power to appoint its own staff. Thus I remember that in my second year at Toronto one of the colleges appointed a young Englishman with a *doctorat d'université* to a full professor.

In practice, the system was established by the spirit of compromise often considered the essence of the Oxbridge tradition. Each college had in fact a *liberum veto* on teaching matters. No courses could be adopted if one of the colleges objected. Historically, I understand, this arrangement was arrived at to accommodate the Catholic St. Michael College. The Catholic Church was very much distrusted and disliked in the nineteenth century, and the residue of that mistrust and dislike were still present during my time in Toronto.

Graduate studies were another victim of the college system. For the old Anglophile professors, graduate studies were "American," therefore unimportant. "A good Honors BA should be enough," I often heard, chiefly from old chaps who had a good Honors BA. During my time, the pressure to establish graduate studies grew stronger and stronger. It came from people like me who had worked hard to acquire a PhD. But St. Michael College founded a graduate program, the Pontifical Institute of Medieval Studies. The leading scholar there was the famous French philosopher and historian Étienne Gilson, who came to Toronto just before the war. The colleges gave in with a perfect "Torontovengian" (the term coined apparently by Gilson) compromise: "Yes, you can teach a graduate course, but as an extra course. That is, you can teach it for free."

I did teach (for free) an introductory graduate course on the history of Old French literature. The circumstances of obtaining this position were rather sad. A young British woman, whose name I have forgotten, was hired by St. Michael College. I met her a couple of times, and she impressed me as bright and knowledgeable. Suddenly, before Christmas, I was called by the head of St. Michael and asked to teach her course because she had left Toronto. Apparently she became ill, saw a doctor, and was told that she had terminal cancer. She went to Switzerland to die.

Among the many people I met at St. Michael was the young, smart, but obviously quite crazy Marshall McLuhan. He was not yet the "famous theoretician." When I met him he was an outspoken assistant professor of English. The undergraduates loved to read his book *The Mechanical Bride* (New York, 1951), a series of reproductions of newspaper pages and especially advertisements, with funny and cynical comments. The book's subtitle, *Folklore of Industrial Man*, shows the author's pretentiousness. Sometime later McLuhan became, for a while, a world figure. He was famous for his concepts of media, global village, "industrial man," and so on. His fame ended as suddenly as it started.

But, to my mind, McLuhan was a precursor of the theory approach. One considers any problem in the light of a preconceived concept, which then becomes a "critical theory." This approach uses certain new general ideas ("theories") as if they were applicable to any problem, just as the Marxist or Freudian ideas of yesterday were applied. Thus, for example, if you wish to study medieval monastic women's communities, you pick up a book on the anthropology of nineteenth-century women's groups in Indonesia. The book thus becomes the "theory." These anthropological findings are less complex, and they substitute for a historical analysis. The simple application of such critical theories to historical studies—which coincided with the waning of Marxism and Freudianism among intellectuals—has compromised and trivialized much academic research and study, in the humanities at least. Lately, such new critical methods have become less ubiquitous, and their end is, perhaps, in sight.

PAUL

Soon after settling in Toronto, we sold our house in Vancouver and bought a small house at the foot of Casa Loma, Toronto's Romantic nineteenth-century castle. We then started to plan to have another child. When Eve was born the doctors had made clear that we could not have another natural child. I talked about these family matters with a colleague of mine, a priest from St. Michael's named Bondy. He told me that the Ontario Children's Aid Society, both the Protestant and Catholic branches, had recently been thoroughly reorganized and that we should talk to them about adopting a child.

At the beginning of 1961, we visited the society and were impressed by a social worker there, a Miss Lecourt. We discussed at length the kind of a child we would like. Miss Lecourt said immediately that in view of our Anna and Eve, it should be a boy. She also told us that, generally speaking, boys were more difficult to place, for everyone prefers a "nice blue-eyed blonde girl." She easily persuaded us that we should aim at a child a little more difficult to place. In those old days in Toronto, only a 100 percent "Indo-European" child was considered easily adoptable. It is difficult to believe that this was only a little more than fifty years ago.

The social worker came to visit our house to see whether there was enough space for another child, and probably to verify that both parents were in favor of adoption. She gave me a truly hard examination without Yolande being present. This was the new spirit of the reorganized Ontario Children's Aid Society, about which Father Bondy had talked so eloquently. Later, during the next round of conversations, she told us that she had a particular boy in mind for us.

After several days of discussions, Miss Lecourt told us to come to her office and bring Anna and Eve with us. That was in March 1961. We came to her office, and a few minutes later she appeared with our son, a boy of a Japanese father and a French Canadian mother. He was beautifully dressed in new clothes. "C'est lui," she said, make up your mind. Both the parents and the daughters were very happy, and we said yes almost immediately. On the way home, we had to stop in a department store to buy all sorts of necessary things for our new son, who had nothing except the fancy clothing that he wore. Before we got our son we had decided to call him Paul Adam. I, of course, was pushing for Adam Paul, but Yolande, perhaps not erroneously, decided that having Adam and Eve in one family would not be wise.

As soon as we arrived at home, we took a photo: Anna, Eve, and Paul in our garden on Davenport Road. We still have it. Eve is beaming at her *petit frère*, and Anna was so excited that she is ready to cry from joy. Paul was four months old when he came to us. He was quite used to the company of grownups, for he spent the time between birth and adoption in a Italian immigrant home. As often happened, the Italian *mammas*, to increase the family income, would take in foster children and cook dinners for young Italian immigrants. Miss Lecourt told us that all the boarders were crying when she came to pick up little "Daniel."

Paul settled in with us outwardly rather easily, but there were some difficulties. He often woke early in the morning and cried. The only way to calm him was to dress him, put him in the stroller, and go out for long walks. Otherwise he was quite happy and well behaved. He, smart fellow, became very attached to his mother. I learned about his attachment the hard way later, during Yolande's temporary absence. Paul had been born on December 12, 1960. In January 1962 we received his birth certificate stating that Peter and Yolande Dembowski are his parents.

Later, Paul studied in Chicago and at the University of San Francisco. There he met Azisti Yuniati, from Indonesia. Yolande went to their wedding in San Francisco in 1986. They have two sons: Arrie, born in 1987, and Alexander, born in 1991. Arrie is the only grandchild who speaks French fluently. Paul and Azisti and their sons are our neighbors in Hyde Park. Paul has always been a good son. He supports me cheerfully in my old age.

POITIERS AND AIX-EN-PROVENCE

In 1964–65 we spent a sabbatical year in the little town of Poitiers. It was easier for a family to live in the provinces, and at Poitiers there is a small medieval institute in which I could work. We invited little Marysia, the eldest daughter of my cousin Anna and her husband, Władek Rodowicz, to stay with us. For me, she expressed, better than anybody else, the feeling shared by all the young people living under the Communist regime: the desire to go abroad. A very popular joke current then in Poland summed up this desire: "Open Sesame, *I want out!*"

Paul's first years with us coincided with the sabbatical in Poitiers. In the fall of 1964, when he was not quite four, he could speak French with us and English with everyone else. After a year in France Paul could not understand a word of English. Proof: Upon our return to Toronto, a neighbor asked him, "Paul, do you want a candy?" This fanatical sweet tooth answered the question with an uncomprehending stare. In Poitiers, Paul was admired by all the women. "Oh, qu'il est mignon!" (Oh, how cute he is!), greeted him every day when he walked with us. In fact, when asked what his name was, he would answer, "Mignon."

I spent the year in Poitiers working on critical editions of the two parts of the *Geste de Blaye*. Five years later I received another sabbatical year. We chose to spend it in another small town, Aix-en-Provence. During that year, I prepared an edition of all the known Old French versions of the *Life of Mary of Egypt* (Geneva, 1977).

TEN

Bernard Weinberg and His University

During my six years at the University of Toronto, I became what could rightly be called a younger scholar. My Berkeley PhD dissertation, published in a well-regarded series by the University of Toronto Press, received several good reviews. One, however, published in *Neophilologus,* a Dutch journal, by an old and important Swedish scholar, was very negative. I was devastated, until I learned that the Swede was an old enemy of Malkiel. Sometime later the editor of *Neophilologus,* understanding the situation, invited me to submit an article of my choice. I did so immediately, an article on *Jourdain de Blaye.* I was working on the critical editions and writing articles and reviews, the latter chiefly for Malkiel's *Romance Philology.* As a result, I began to receive feelers from other universities. In 1964 I was promoted to associate professor with tenure at Toronto.

Nevertheless, I was not particularly happy at the University of Toronto. Though I had problems with the university administration, fundamentally, I believe, I was unhappy with my colleagues. There were, of course, good scholars at the university; however, they did not influence the general atmosphere, which did not encourage serious involvement in scholarly work. I missed Berkeley. My feelings, shared with some younger colleagues, can be illustrated by the following anecdote. We had organized a unofficial competition for the translation of the beautiful University of Toronto motto taken from Juvenal: "Velut arbor aevo" (As a tree with the passage of time). My contribution to the competition, "Plenty of Deadwood," was appreciated and won some laughs.

And then something important happened. Professor Bernard Weinberg, chair of the Department of Romance Languages at the University of Chicago, came to visit. By then I knew all about this university, for I had received an offer for an assistant professorship from Ruth Webber, chair of the college (undergraduate) section of the Department of Romance Languages. I told Webber that I had already received tenure as an associate professor, and the matter ended.

At Toronto, Weinberg gave a truly inspired lecture: a brilliant *explication de texte* of a difficult poem by Baudelaire. Afterward he had occasion to speak with me. He spoke passionately about his university, where he had received his undergraduate and graduate education. After his sudden and untimely death in 1973, at the age of sixty-four, I wrote a chapter on him for a collection of studies of great members of the Chicago faculty, *Remembering the University of Chicago: Teachers, Scientists, and Scholars* (Chicago, 1991). Here, it suffices to say that he was a world-class scholar and my very good friend.

Sometime after Weinberg's visit, I received a letter from him offering me an associate professorship with tenure at the University of Chicago. I wanted to accept at once, but prudence made me hesitate. This was early 1966. The United States was in Vietnam, and on the campuses students were raising hell. In Chicago there were also racial tensions, and the journalists had exaggerated these tensions in their usual way. The press in general loves bad news, and thrives on it (sorry about that, my journalist grandson, Sebastian Strangio).

I asked, therefore, to visit the campus. I did this on a Friday in the early spring of 1966. I was very well received by Weinberg, who presented me to many of his colleagues and cooked a good dinner (meatless, for he knew that I was an observant Catholic, though he did not know that by then abstinence from meat on Fridays was no longer required). I met the dean, Robert Streeter, who impressed me as being both learned and enthusiastic about learning in spite of his many years as dean, first of the college and later of the Division of Humanities.

All the Chicagoans whom I met during my visit expressed the hope that I would accept the university's offer. Apparently, during my visit the students organized a small sit-in against the military draft, but Weinberg guided me so well that I did not notice it. It was decided that I would give my definitive answer in a few days.

I consulted Malkiel, who wrote to me at once that I should accept the offer *tout de suite* and to accept definitively, without asking for a one-year probationary term. More important for me was, again, the attitude of my wife, and she too was very much in favor of the move. The two most important decisions in my scholarly life, going to Berkeley for the PhD and accepting the University of Chicago's job offer, were greatly influenced by her encouragement. I shall be always grateful to *ma chère* Yolande.

AT HOME IN CHICAGO

In September 1966 we arrived in Chicago, or rather, Hyde Park, a former village incorporated into the City of Chicago at the end of the nineteenth century. Hyde Park, on the South Side, is the seat of the University of Chicago. In September 1966 it looked a little like a liberated city during World War II. At the end of 1950 the university had made the momentous decision to renovate the area, with the collaboration of the city, of course. During the war thousands of poor blacks had come to the South Side to work in the wartime industries. The area became overcrowded and badly run-down. The university had a hard time convincing faculty members and their families to live near campus, and attracting new faculty like me.

The urban renewal of Hyde Park was the first, or one of the first, such actions undertaken by a private university. It consisted of buying outright the deteriorated buildings, demolishing them, and building new living quarters in their stead. Much of the Hyde Park of today consists of those "renewed" or newly built living quarters. Urban renewal was a difficult and certainly controversial action. Weinberg explained to me the origins and strategies of urban renewal. He found it absolutely necessary for the survival of the university. I know that he was right.

The leftist intelligentsia, always present on every campus, held "simpler" opinions. They termed urban renewal "Negro Removal" and considered it a "racist" policy. But I know that many of the most vociferous critics moved away into "safer" districts. As is usual in such cases, the critics did not offer alternatives. The fact is that urban renewal did "remove" the poor people from their rundown homes, but there was no racist intent. Now, many years after urban renewal, more than 50 percent of Hyde Park's population is black, primarily middle class. I still read in "progressive" journals that urban renewal was a tragedy and a crime.

As I said, we arrived in Hyde Park in September 1966. Yolande had come to Chicago earlier and found an apartment on Hyde Park Boulevard. We lived there until the end of March 1967, when we bought our present town house, on Kenwood Avenue, with the money from the sale of our Toronto house.

Many of my new colleagues celebrated our buying the house with a huge housewarming party. Urban renewal had succeeded in attracting private investors, and our house was one of the earliest ones built by a private contractor. Both our colleagues and we were happy that we had invested in the renewed neighborhood.

During our years in Hyde Park we found that the mixed population has lived in peace. We also found, when urban renewal was over, that most people were satisfied that the university had carried out the risky and costly project, even if they did not say it out loud, for fear of sounding "reactionary." At the beginning of our stay, the professors who traveled and lectured to the alumni of the university were often met with an anxious question, "How is the neighborhood?" For the past ten years at least, the question is rarely asked. And if it is, our usual response is, "Fine, we can hardly afford to live in it."

Neither I nor the rest of the family has ever regretted coming to Chicago. We felt at home from the start, and, unlike Toronto, nobody asked us to "understand" Chicago. Anna, Eve, and Paul received their primary and secondary education here and have made many lifelong friends. Paul quickly made friends among both white and black children. I remember one day he brought home a little black girl and said to his mother, "Maman, viens voir ma blonde" (Come see my blonde; *blonde* in Canadian French means both "blonde" and "girlfriend"). I also remember overhearing the conversation between the very young Paul and his friends. "Paul, are you white, or are you black?" As Paul kept silent, the little boy declared, "If you aren't white and if you aren't black, you're nothing." I went into a panic about Paul's self-identification, but he answered, "I'm Canadian," which seemed to satisfy his friend. Children are nominalists; they must have a name to solve the problem.

Anna, Eve, and Paul attended the public primary schools in Hyde Park. But the public secondary schools were bad: too many gangs and not enough learning. That was the situation in Hyde Park and in the rest of Chicago. Therefore, Anna and Eve went to University of Chicago Laboratory High School, and Paul was sent to the Jesuits at St. Ignatius Preparatory College. The situation has improved somewhat in Chicago, for one of Paul's sons, Arrie, went to a good public magnet high school. Alex, however, attended a Catholic high school in the neighborhood, Mount Carmel.

For me, the University of Chicago was everything that I had sought after deciding to become an academic. The majority of my colleagues are competent, and many of them are, in fact, outstanding researchers in their fields. I have made many good friends and colleagues at Chicago, far too many to be mentioned here. The Round Table at the Quadrangle Club, the faculty club, where I have been eating lunch, at the same table, for more than forty-five years, would take many pages to describe. Indeed, the University of Chicago is a rich place, and I have thrived in it.

The university is also a wise place. I have never heard in Chicago the eternal and mindless discussions (so common in Vancouver and Toronto) of the supposed conflict between teaching and research. Such discussions are indeed mindless, because one has to do both good teaching and "healthy" research. If there are bad teachers among the good researchers (I have hardly met any), their bad teaching has not been caused by devoting too much time to research but by some other personal failing. On the other hand, teachers in a good university must be involved in research, or at least must have an abounding interest in their subject matter, to maintain their desire to teach well. I found that the University of Chicago encouraged me to improve my research activities, which certainly helped me to teach well. I published a good deal, and I also received many good teaching evaluations. I have many accomplished and grateful former students. Those achievements give me real satisfaction in my old age.

DEAN OF STUDENTS AND THE SIT-IN

One day, at the end of the spring quarter of 1968, I had just finished teaching my graduate course on the history of Romance languages when I was surprised to find Edward H. Levi, the provost and president-elect of the university, waiting for me outside my door. I knew him, of course: one of the beauties of the University of Chicago is that it is relatively small and most of the faculty members know each other. I had met Levi often, usually at lunch in the Quadrangle Club, and I considered him my friend. I waited to hear what he had to say. Without preliminaries, he said that the Division of the Humanities needed a dean of students as of October 1, 1968, and he wanted me to accept that position. I was so flabbergasted that I accepted right away.

Levi was certainly one of the most intelligent persons I have ever known. He always seemed to me to be outspoken, witty, and kind. For many years we cherished his friendship and that of his wife, Kate, who was lively, intelligent, and very friendly to Yolande and me. Levi was fourteen years my senior. He died in 2000, after serving as U.S. attorney general under President Gerald Ford. One of the sad aspects of old age is that we lose many good friends in the last years of our life. As G. K. Chesterton said, we live largely "in the Republic of the Dead."

Accepting the dean of students position led to serious repercussions in my life. I served two academic years, 1968–69 and 1969–70, in that position. The first year was characterized by strong student unhappiness and anxiety throughout the United States and in many other parts of the world. This state of mind resulted in rebellion and unrest in our university. The first instance took place in November 1968: a protest against the installation of the new president of the university, Edward Levi. Like many political events in those days, the assumption of the presidency by Levi was not the real cause but merely a pretext for the protest. The word for *pretext* used by the rebelling students was "the issue."

I remember well that first student demonstration, which took place in front of Rockefeller Chapel, during the installation ceremony of the new president. The students, gathered in considerable numbers, were strangely excited. I still recall young women trembling, as if expecting an attack by the Cossacks. That night the students, led by the Students for a Democratic Society (SDS)—a left organization that flourished in the mid- to late 1960s in opposition to American participation in the Vietnam War—tried, and largely succeeded, to interrupt the civic dinner in honor of the new president.

Levi did not take action against the students, and the real event came at the beginning of the next winter quarter in 1969. Some 150 students occupied the Administration Building, where, incidentally, the dean's office was located. The "issue" used by SDS was not the Vietnam War but the defense of a female professor of sociology who had not been promoted to tenure. In fact, the sit-in was the exploitation of various forms of public unhappiness and frustration on the part of SDS. If I underscore the Leninist tactics of the organizers, it stems from being close to the action and hearing the leaders bragging about their ability to organize the students into a "revolutionary group."

Levi did not call the police to free the Administration Building. Instead, he kept in touch with the faculty through various meetings, and he waited. After about two weeks, the occupying students left the building, and since they were young Chicago intellectuals, they published a final "proclamation of defeat." This declaration insisted again that "the issue was not the issue," for the real purpose (or "issue") was to create a revolutionary situation. The end of the sit-in was a relief for me. During the sit-in I had to be a witness for the university. And I had to attend all the meetings called by Levi. I had no time to sleep.

I was very happy that after two difficult years of being dean, I was granted a sabbatical. We spent 1970–71 in Aix-en-Provence. I realized, especially during the sit-in, that I was totally at home at Chicago and in the United States. I respected Canada, and I was grateful to Canada for ending my statelessness. But I knew that I would spend the rest of my life in the United States, and therefore, in June 1974, I became an American citizen. Like many foreign born, I am an American patriot.

MY WORK

In 1971, after my sabbatical year, we returned to a much more peaceful University of Chicago. I threw myself into my work. I realize that it is difficult to talk to nonacademics about academic work. Simply, it consists of teaching and research, that is, studying your specialty, which results in the publication of books, articles, and reviews. The most important thing about my work, both teaching and research, is that I have always loved it. This feeling has been shared at the University of Chicago by many of my colleagues and friends. We often talk about this love. A common expression among younger scholars at Chicago in my early days there was, "It's true that I make less than a truck driver, but, by God, I love the work." I remember once that my very good friend Charles Wegener (who died in 2002) said after he had given a public lecture, "Imagine, I even got paid for it." I consider my enjoyment in my work a real blessing in my life.

Yolande also loved her work. She taught French at Loyola University from the time of our arrival in Chicago until her retirement in 1986, at the age of sixty. She was deeply interested in the literature she taught and drew a lot of satisfaction from her work. Her enjoyment in teaching encouraged my own positive attitude.

Looking back on my life, I must say that I am happy about my academic publications. I have published several critical editions of old texts. And one of the pleasures of old age is to find references to my works in the publications of my younger colleagues.

But, of course, I had other duties to perform at the university. In addition to two years of serving as dean of students, I was chair of the Department of Romance Languages and Literatures, first between 1976 and 1983 and then again in the 1986–87 school year. More important, perhaps, we were resident masters in Snell and Hitchcock Halls, undergraduate residences, between 1972 and 1979. Yolande was fully recognized as an active partner in that job, perhaps in part because Snell Hall was inhabited by women students.

Although creating the job of resident master had been considered for some time, the actual establishment of that position largely resulted from the post–sit-in discussions of undergraduate life. The resident masters have assistants, usually graduate students or junior faculty. I encouraged my various colleagues to come to our weekly suppers and talk to the students about their work. Yolande took care of the supper itself, cooked by our neighbor, the cheerful Mrs. Hayek. Some fifteen students from both houses were invited each week. Coffee and dessert were served to anybody who cared to come. The usual group of big eaters (males) came after dinner to finish off the leftovers. The Wednesday evenings were also a success because neither Hitchcock nor Snell had a dining room. The students had to cook for themselves in the basement kitchen.

Because of this arrangement, the two residence halls housed a considerable number of students who kept kosher. Thus from time to time we organized strictly kosher dinners, carefully supervised by Steven Feldman, an undergraduate who became our good friend and remains so today. We made other lasting friends as resident masters, among them, Michael Karluk and John McLees.

Eve and Anna seemed to like living in Hitchcock Hall, and Paul certainly did. He played (illegally) on one of the basketball teams.

Hitchcock officially had two teams, Hitchcock East and Hitchcock West, but the students of Asian descent created another team, Hitchcock Far East, and I believe Paul played on that one.

We left the mastership in 1979. I went to Princeton as a member of the Institute for Advanced Study, where I wrote a book on Froissart's long poem called *Meliador* (Lexington, 1983). In 1995, when I was seventy years old, I officially retired from the university. My title at that time was Distinguished Service Professor of French. I taught part-time for the next several years, and to this day I continue to spend considerable time in my library study.

ELEVEN

Les Eboulements

Our summer place in Les Eboulements, a small village perched on the high bank of the St. Lawrence about ninety miles east of Quebec City, was very important in our lives. In order to relate how we acquired that lovely home for numerous summers, I must go back in time.

In 1964–65 we were spending a sabbatical year in Poitiers, and we planned to take the boat from Montreal. An old friend of Yolande's, Yvon Gauthier, a psychiatrist, told us that he had just bought a farmhouse in Les Eboulements. He said that the house had been unoccupied for several years and that he and his family (his wife, Elisabeth, and their five children) were hesitant to live there during the next summer. If we wished, we could spend a few weeks there. We accepted the proposition, and thus began our love adventure with this place that lasted for some forty-five years.

From the village one can see the majestic St. Lawrence River, the Ile aux Coudres, and the ferry that leaves from the Lower Village of Les Eboulements. The view of the St. Lawrence is breathtaking. On a sunny day one can see the south shore of the river, and on the northern and northwestern side lie the mountains. The climate is fiercely cold in winter and pleasantly cool in summer.

In fact, the region was discovered, in pre–air-conditioning times, by tourists, chiefly Americans, from the East Coast. They came to the region of La Malbaie (some twenty-five miles north-east of Les Eboulements) to avoid the summer heat. Many of the local people, who are exclusively French Canadian, bear Scottish names. These are the descendants of British soldiers disbanded in Charlevoix at the end of the eighteenth century. All the inhabitants are quite sensitive to the beauty of the landscape. They often talk about living in a place *en belle vue*. From our first stay in Les Eboulements, we wanted to return.

We spent the next forty-three happy summers in Les Eboulements, and we always had a pleasant relationship with our neighbors. Our stays in Les Eboulements not only restored our souls but also kept us in touch with Yolande's homeland.

We began to build our house in Les Eboulements in 1968. Early that summer I drove the family from Chicago to Les Eboulements, and I returned to Chicago to work. At the end of August, I went back to Les Eboulements to find that Yolande had managed to have the basic parts of our house constructed. Ernest Tramblay, Lomer's brother-in-law, hired a few people, most of them Tramblays, the predominant family name in Les Eboulements and its district. They had built the foundations, the walls, and the roof of our house. Secondhand windows had been installed, and a secondhand kitchen stove served for cooking and heat. Ernest did not follow Yolande's plans, but I still became known as *le mari de la femme architecte* (husband of the woman architect). We lived almost as if in a tent for the first three summers.

The main idea for the construction of our summer house was that we would pay for it without borrowing a cent and that I would do most of the work. In my school days in Poland, we had classes in "handicraft" (*roboty ręczne*); boys did the carpentry, and the girls cooked and sewed. During many summers in Les Eboulements, I improved on the skills acquired at school. First, I insulated the house. Next, I covered the walls with pine siding and finished most of the inside of the house, all with my own hands. The work was very gratifying. To this day, I brag about my avocation (carpentry) more than I brag about my vocation (scholarship). Later we built covered porches on the eastern and southern sides.

At first I could not spend the entire summer in Les Eboulements because of my academic work. But from about my sixtieth birthday on, my study in Les Eboulements was well furnished and my computer kept me in contact with the university library's catalogs, and so on, and I could remain through the summer. I developed a steady routine: in the morning, academic work; in the afternoon, physical work. One morning I heard my two old neighbors talking below my open window. One said (in French, *bien sûr*), "He does pretty good work [*ouvrage* = carpentry], but he does not do anything in the morning." I was flattered. I realized that it is impossible to explain to the good countrymen of Les Eboulements that sitting in front of a computer is "work."

As soon as the house was finished, I started to attend to the grounds. We bought a small tractor mower and constructed a fence around our parcel of land. Since I found that the driving from Chicago to Les Eboulements (1,100 miles) was becoming more and more tiring, we decided to buy another car and keep the old one in Les Eboulements over the winter. This required a garage.

The garage was built by the old mason, Emile Tramblay, and his helper. I, of course, worked with them. Sometime after the construction of the garage, we decided to build a large room adjacent to the north side of the garage. The government of Quebec is extremely fond of rules, regulations, and old and new laws. The natives of the *belle province* are extremely well versed in circumventing those rules. But *les étrangers* like us had to obey them. According to these rules, we could not build anything that could be considered another dwelling because agricultural land was protected (our *indivis* was, in fact, part of the agricultural land). This time, I avoided Emile and worked with the former owner of the farm, Lomer. For legal reasons, we called this additional room a "tool shed" and received a *permis de construction*. Once you have a permit, nobody bothers you. We insulated the room and put two beds and an electric heater in it, along with a small washroom in the garage space, adjacent to the "tool shed." It became a comfortable room, and my brother Bronek spent many happy weeks there when he visited. Arrie fabricated a handsome crucifix so that Bronek could celebrate Mass in his room.

YOLANDE'S ILLNESS AND DEATH

All good things must end, and our long love affair with our place in Les Eboulements came to a sudden halt. One night in July 2009 I was awakened by Yolande falling out of bed. She could speak, and though she understood what was going on around her, she could not explain her fall. She could not move her legs. The next morning I took her to the Baie-Saint-Paul hospital. I could not learn anything from the doctors or nurses about her condition. After a few days, we were told that she had to be transported to the Hôpital de l'Enfant Jésus in Quebec City to have a brain scan, for the hospital in Baie-Saint-Paul, like many other small hospitals in the province, was not equipped with sophisticated instruments.

The hospital was incredibly crowded, and Yolande was put on a stretcher in the corridor. There were many patients like her from other small hospitals in the eastern part of the province. Yolande spent three days in the Quebec City hospital. Again, I could not get any information about her condition. Finally, on the third day, I forcefully buttonholed a doctor, who told me only that the patient should be sent back to Baie-Saint-Paul, where in due time she would undergo a psychiatric examination. Indeed, after a few days she was examined by a visiting psychiatrist, who confirmed, as I knew quite well, that "Mme Dembowski has no psychotic symptoms." The psychiatrist's visit made me suspect that the Hôpital de l'Enfant Jésus had failed to discover that she had suffered a stroke.

In Les Eboulements we soon suffered another, lesser misfortune: Victor, our dear cat Victor, native of Charlevoix and a well-behaved frequent flyer from Chicago to Quebec, had disappeared. Soon I discovered that he had been eaten by the coyotes that had recently established themselves in our district. Our cat was one of their first victims. We were sorry about Victor. For me, his death, irrationally, weakened the false sense of security that for so many years I had had about Les Eboulements. His death instilled in me a new sense of the impermanence of things, which made abandoning our summer place perhaps a little easier.

We went back to Chicago earlier than usual. We settled down and, of course, immediately adopted another cat, a pure American female, but we gave her a French Canadian name, Minouche. Yolande was quite well now but had difficulty walking. Outside the house, she used a wheelchair.

One night in March 2010, during Eve's visit to Chicago, I again found Yolande on the floor of our bedroom. I could not lift her myself, so I woke Eve, and we put her back in the bed. The next day she was taken to the emergency room at the University of Chicago Hospital. After a night there, she was taken to the Department of Neurology, run by my former student and a former Hitchcock resident, Dr. Christopher Gomez. He told us that Yolande had suffered a *second* stroke. This confirmed that her illness some months earlier in Quebec had indeed been a stroke.

This second stroke was more severe than the first, and, according to the doctors, it was accompanied by other pathological neurological developments. Again, Yolande could not move her legs. After a few days in the hospital, she was transferred to a nursing home, where she began the slow process of recovery. Soon she came home, and after a while she could move about the house by herself, with the aid of a walker. Her physical state became stable, with only slight improvements. Later, in 2013, the symptoms of Alzheimer's disease became more and more obvious.

In the late summer of 2014, Yolande's situation stabilized. She was mostly bedridden but could move around the house using a walker. She was quite weak, and she slept most of the time. Her mental capacities diminished considerably, and she was often confused. In the morning, Carmen, a pleasant young woman, stayed with her. At 2:30, after lunch at the Faculty Club and a swim, I was home to spend the rest of the day with Yolande. In the evening our daughter Anna came to chat with her mother. Since Yolande suffered from sleep apnea, Anna put the breathing apparatus on her mother before bed. Later she shared a bottle of red wine with me. She poured, which made my life free from temptations. We often talked about Yolande.

Alas, Yolande died peacefully and at home on September 8, 2014, 61 years to the day of our first meeting.

THE END OF LES EBOULEMENTS AND BRIEF CONCLUDING THOUGHTS ON OLD AGE, ETC.

Eve was again with us in the summer of 2010, and I went to Les Eboulements with Anna. Some time ago we had made a promise to sell our house to the daughter of my recently deceased friend Lomer Bouchard. We proceeded with this plan, and thus in August 2010 our beloved summer place became the property of Martine Bouchard and Dany Hammond, her husband. We were happy about that: Martine was born on our farm. She and her husband take loving care of the chalet. They recently sent a photo of the house nicely maintained and tastefully repainted. But an important chapter in our lives was closed.

Yolande's death, the "loss" of Les Eboulements, and the end of our annual peregrinations from Chicago to the rural world of Quebec made me realize that I am, indeed, old. This made me think about my past and made me eager to write about my past. I realized that my past was "interesting." I lived in historically "important times." I come from an interesting family, characterized by seriousness and deep involvement in either left-wing politics or the Christian faith or both.

In North America I started my life at the bottom, and I became a successful immigrant. I adapted completely and happily to life in my new country, the United States. I had a fine and deeply satisfying professional academic career. But, above all, I have been blessed with a good family, with a loving wife and loving children and grandchildren. Thus I have much to be thankful for, and this is my main sentiment at the realization of my old age.

Nobody is prepared to become old. An inscription on a t-shirt that I saw recently sums it up well: "Old Age Comes at an Inconvenient Time." It is not only a good joke, but like many good jokes, it is also an expression of a deeper psychological truth. The full realization that one is old comes with the deeper realization of the finite character of life. Contrary to what younger people might think, the realization of old age is neither automatic nor simple. Usually, it requires a shock, and we had two of them.

The reader has probably guessed that "Etc." in the title of this section is a polite synonym for "death," this companion of old age. I would like to share here some of my thoughts on this usually unmentionable subject. I wish to make them as simple and as clear as possible. It would be a falsification of my whole life if these thoughts were not expressed in religious language. For the fact is that I have always considered death in religious terms. And I have always been religious. There is no doubt in my mind that I inherited my Catholic faith chiefly from my mother, whose religious faith was very much influenced and deepened by her association with two converts, Janina Landy Dembowska and her sister Zofia Landy (Sister Katarzyna of the Laski convent).

From the earliest time in my life, I witnessed in my mother a deep religious faith and a genuine practice of goodwill toward others. She loved us all, and I belive that I inherited this capacity for love, which is the main aspect of religion. My brother Bronek, a good priest and a good bishop, also strengthened me in my religious beliefs.

Religious conviction is not simply faith in something that you cannot see. It is a combination of other attitudes, that is, virtues. In the words of Saint Paul, "So faith, hope and love endure. These are the great three, and the greatest of them is love" (1 Corinthians 13:13). Love is, so to speak, the engine of faith and hope. I discovered in my old age that in this trinity of faith, hope, and love, the middle term has become very important. I hope, I wish, I expect, that the virtue of hope will remain with me to the end.

If you ask me who or what is the object of my faith, hope, and love, I will answer: Jesus the Christ. And if you ask, "Can you love somebody who died some two thousand years ago?," my answer would be yes, for I am a medievalist, and I love many historical figures. I love Saint Peter and Saint Francis, I love Roland, I love Joan of Arc, and I love many people long dead. But my most important love is the love for my mother, who, as I said, instilled in me the capacity for love and who has been dead for more than seventy years now.

The Catholic tradition has always acknowledged a strong connection between faith, hope, and love and the realization of one's mortality. An important prayer to the Mother of Jesus, to intervene on our behalf, is a paraphrase of the biblical angelic greeting of Mary: "Hail Mary, full of grace, the Lord is with you" (Luke 1:28), which is followed by the greetings from her kin Elizabeth: "Blessed are you among women and blessed is the fruit of thy womb, Jesus" (Luke 1:42). Originally that was the entire prayer. Later, probably in the fourteenth century, following the time of the Black Death, something very important was added: "Holy Mary, Mother of God, pray for us sinners now and in the hour of our death." And this "now and in the hour of our death" (*nunc in hora mortis nostrae*), which I have probably uttered at least twenty-five thousand times, certainly affected my concept of my own end of life.

Like life, death is a gift of God. Nobody said it better than my friend Saint Francis of Assisi. His famous poem "The Canticle of the Creatures" praises the Creator through his creations. The poet begins with our Brother Sun, our Sister Moon, and our Sister Earth and ends with the following: "Laudato si' mi' Signore per sora nostra morte corporale" (Be blessed my Lord through our sister the bodily death). Death is, of course, inevitable. Saint Francis adds right after the praise of our sister, the bodily death: "la quella nullu homo vivente po skapare" (from whom no living man can escape). Since death is the gift of God, it should be accepted with a thoughtful and a hopeful submission, and that is what I have been attempting to do.

At the *suprema hora*, as the pagan Romans called the moment of death, I expect to say with hope, "God be with you," and someone, I hope, will respond with faith and love, "And with your spirit." And then we will say, "Amen," for this beautiful Hebrew word means "so be it."

INDEX

Names in quotation marks represent pseudonyms used in the Underground.

PETER F. DEMBOWSKI is a Distinguished Service Professor Emeritus at the University of Chicago. He is the author of *Christians in the Warsaw Ghetto: An Epitaph for the Unremembered* (2005), also published by the University of Notre Dame Press.